NORWAY
revolts against
THE NAZIS

by

JACOB WORM-MULLER
former Professor of History at Oslo University

LINDSAY DRUMMOND
6 BUCKINGHAM STREET
W.C. 2

First published 1941

PRINTED IN GREAT BRITAIN BY
STEPHEN AUSTIN AND SONS, LTD., HERTFORD

CONTENTS

ILLUSTRATIONS

CHAPTER I

The Invasion and Quisling

TO understand what happened to Norway on the 9th April, 1940
and to understand the reactions of the people at that
time, one must first realize that the general feeling in the
Scandinavian countries was then very similar to that which
is still current among many persons in the United States.
I refer to the feeling summed up in the phrase 'It can't
happen here'.

The great majority of Norwegian people really could not
believe that the Germans would ever attack and suppress the
nordic people, who desired only to live in peace and to carry
on their own way of life—one devoted to national culture,
economic progress, social justice, and international understanding.

We failed to realize, therefore, that this new war vitally
concerned us. We failed to realize that what broke out in
1939, was not just a war but a world civil war, a world
revolution, which threatened everything we held sacred, our
democratic institutions, our national ideals, our laws and
constitution. We did not comprehend that what really
menaced the world was the complete nazification of all
mankind. We did not at once realize what nazism really
meant, that these men were only gangsters, as the German
negotiator in Norway, Delbrügge, the Regierungspräsident,
informed us by a slip of the tongue, when he said: '*Wir sind
eine internationale Bande.*'

It is a terrible tragedy that apparently no nation can learn
its lesson from what befalls other nations. Each country must
experience invasion and disaster at first hand before it can
believe them possible or grasp their full horrors. This is one
of the secret weapons of the dictators. They succeeded
because they took their victims one by one. Scholars, perhaps,

can learn from history, but the unfortunate thing is that the citizen of the modern democracies usually understands, too late, not only the lessons of the past but the lessons of the contemporary events. And so most people in Norway did not for a moment believe that we should suffer the same fate as Poland and Czechoslovakia. We had no quarrels with the Germans, no national minority or frontier problems. Why then, should we fear attack?

Consequently when the Germans did treacherously attack us in April, we were taken completely by surprise, and utterly shocked and mystified. There were some traitors of course, but they were not persons in key positions nor were they nearly as many as the world at first believed. Far more serious than any treachery was the factor of confusion, of bewildered astonishment that such a thing could happen in Norway.

The American journalist Leland Stowe discredited our people at the beginning, by telling the world that the inhabitants of Oslo looked with indifference upon the entry of the German soldiers, regarding it as simply an extraordinary spectacle. I happened to see the invasion from the same place as Mr. Stowe, but I had quite a different impression of the reaction of the people. They were not indifferent, but completely bewildered and paralysed. It was like a nightmare.

At this moment, one of the darkest of our modern history, Vidkun Quisling appeared, and proclaimed himself Prime Minister. The situation was completely changed. For many years Quisling had tried without any success to create a party called *Nasjonal Samling* (National Union); now within a few hours he succeeded in creating a real national union *against* himself. He was a traitor, but at the same time he did us the greatest service possible, for he united the people and made any negotiations with the Germans impossible. At the time of invasion our people were divided by parties and class-warfare, but at once nearly every Norwegian was agreed about one thing: we would never accept the traitor. As a result of this complete opposition to Quisling, everything was in a state of chaos within a few days. Most of the government officials did not appear in their departments, labour in Oslo was almost in revolt and threatened to come out on strike, and business, trade, and commerce were on the point of collapse. Quisling's so-called government did nothing; only three persons dared to join him openly; most of the others kept away from him. One of them, an officer, joined the army in protest, and the present minister of police, Jonas Lie, tried to procure an alibi for himself, by taking part in the war for a few days.

For the German High Command, Quisling proved a terrible disappointment and they very soon realized that his influence was nil. When one of the Germans asked the clerk of the Parliament how many members Quisling had in the *Storting* (Parliament), and the clerk replied: 'None at all,' he refused at first to believe it. And they were even more astonished when they read through the list of his followers and found out that most of these people were still going to school.

Quisling's prestige amongst the Germans vanished rapidly. When on Friday, the 12th April, he suddenly dismissed the head of the police in Oslo the Germans plainly informed the latter that he need not take any notice. They told the President of the City Council the same thing in the evening: 'Ignore it, it does not matter in the least.' They were so anxious to get rid of him as soon as possible, that on Monday, the 15th April, within the space of one hour, they bluntly threw him and his storm troopers out from their headquarters at the Hotel Continental. On the same day the Administrative Council, to which I shall refer in a moment, was established.

From now on until the middle of August Quisling almost disappeared from the public eye. Instead of being Prime Minister, he now became Commissioner for Demobilization; an utterly obscure title, which in itself completely exposed his treachery. He was daily in contact with the German authorities, but he was extremely unpopular and became more and more ridiculous.

CHAPTER 2

The Administrative Council takes over

THE Constitution of Norway was established by the National Assembly at Eidsvold on 17th May, 1814, and was still in existence when the invasion took place, but a great many amendments had been made during the hundred and twenty-six years which had elapsed since its inception. The Constitution was built upon the three-power principle which asserts that there shall be no overlapping between the Executive power: the King and the Government; the Legislative power: the Storting, consisting of 150 members; and the Judiciary power: the Supreme Court, and all other courts.

For many years the Labour Party had been the largest party in the Storting. It would not have constituted a majority over the combined representatives of the Conservative, the Liberal-Radical, and the Farmers' Parties, but these parties never united. Since 1935 the Labour Party had been in office with Mr. Nygaardsvold as Prime Minister.

When the Germans invaded Norway, the Government and the President of the Storting, Mr. Hambro, immediately decided that the King, the Government, and the Parliament should leave the capital, early in the morning of 9th April, and move to Hamar—a communication centre north-east of Oslo—in order to deliberate in freedom. It was most fortunate for Norway that this decision was made. This was no flight but a brilliant strategic move. If the governmental authorities had remained in Oslo, the Germans, with one stroke, would have captured them all and thus have broken down all possible resistance. At Hamar the Nygaardsvold Government resigned, in order to give way to a National Government, but the Parliament unanimously requested them to remain in office. It was, at that moment, impossible to change the Government, and moreover it had the confidence of a solid majority. The Prime Minister accepted the vote of confidence and declared that the Government should be reinforced by the appointment of new Ministers, representing the other Parties. This was done by the creation of three new offices for Ministers without Portfolio.

The deliberations of the Parliament, at the afternoon meeting that same day, were interrupted by the news that German soldiers were approaching Hamar in motor buses. So the Storting hurriedly left for Elverum, farther north-east, where the Parliament was to hold its last meeting. Here the Storting took the most far-reaching decisions which saved the Kingdom of Norway, because they provided for all eventualities which might arise during the course of the war. They created three appointments for Ministers without Portfolio, and by this action the Labour Party was transformed into a National Government. Then the Storting, unanimously and without any discussion, gave the Government full power to take any steps and to make any decisions which they might find necessary under war-time conditions. The President of the Storting declared that the Government had the necessary international authority to make any decisions, even if they had to move to a foreign country. The Storting thus laid the constitutional foundation for the Government's fight for the liberation of Norway from London. After this it was unanimously agreed to adjourn the Storting until it could meet again in complete freedom.

It was clear to all the members of the Storting that there could be no meetings under the existing military conditions, so the members of Parliament left Elverum and tried to return to their various constituencies. Meanwhile the Government followed the Army and moved, under heavy aerial bombardment and between parachute troops, into the Gudbrand Valley; then farther on to Molde, where they remained until the evacuation of Aandalsnes; then on to Tromsö, in the far north, until finally, on 7th June, the King and the Government, to their deepest sorrow, were forced to leave Norway on the British cruiser *Devonshire*, in order to establish themselves in London as the legal Government, with the firm resolve to fight until victory is won.

From the 9th April the Government had been unable to perform their duties in Oslo and the surrounding occupied districts, because all communications were cut. It was, therefore, necessary to form a temporary Administrative body. In the existing chaos the German High Command, the German Minister, the Trades Union Congress, and the Norwegian Associations of Producers (Shipping, Industry, Commerce, and Farming), were all equally anxious to establish some sort of order.

The Administrative Council, appointed by the Supreme Court, consisted of seven members, mostly outstanding officials, under the chairmanship of Mr. Christensen, the Governor of Oslo and the province of Akershus. It was not a political body, but only a civilian administration, a civil institution of stewardship with no political function, intended, during the German occupation, to function as long as the King and the Government were absent from the capital and the surrounding districts. It was pointed out that the Department for Foreign Affairs and the Department of Defence were excluded from the new arrangement, and therefore the Administrative Council had nothing to do with the conduct of the war. The council was not a government formed in opposition to the King and the legal government, but an emergency institution, appointed by the Supreme Court, which represented the judicial power in the constitution. Later on this act was sanctioned by the Royal Norwegian Government.

Under the constitution of Norway (i.e. before April, 1940), the Supreme Court has no political or constitutional power whatsoever, but the Supreme Court constitutes, in conjunction with certain members of the Storting (the Lag-Ting), the so-called *Riksrett*—the constitutional court of the realm, whose task it is to deliver judgment either against members of the Council of State or against members of the Storting. The Supreme Court has also the right to decide if laws voted by the Storting are constitutional. The judgment of the Supreme

Court is final, and cannot be appealed against or cancelled by the administration. According to the Constitution, the judges cannot be dismissed. In the event of the death of the King, and the heir being a minor, it was the unconditional duty of the Supreme Court to get the Storting convoked after four years. Therefore, the Supreme Court, as supreme power in the State, finding the present extraordinary state of affairs analogous to the situation in the event of the death of the King, made this emergency decision, but the Chief Justice immediately informed the King by telephoning to the Legation in Stockholm, who informed the King at his headquarters in Norway.

There were two different opinions about the emergency decision of the Supreme Court : some people said that the formation of an emergency institution at this moment could only be of advantage to the Germans, who were not certain that the invasion had already succeeded. In this case it was better to have chaos than order. They said: 'If you offer the devil a finger, he will grab the whole hand.' But the overwhelming majority of the inhabitants said: 'This confusion cannot continue. We must stop the disorder and keep things going as usual, and above all we must get rid of Quisling.'

The Administrative Council was hailed with the universal support of the press and public opinion in the occupied regions. Personally I was not very happy about it and was in doubt as to whether it was the right thing to do, but nearly all my friends and people whom I trusted felt as if they had been woken from a nightmare—they had all feared things would be so very much worse.

During the whole of this period the Germans tried to play the part of friends and 'protectors,' according to the instructions they had received on leaving Germany. These instructions, which were found on German soldiers, explained among other things that the Norwegians had a strong national feeling, and that, therefore, everything which might offend their national honour must be avoided, and also that the Norwegians loved their freedom and had a strong feeling of independence, that they reacted strongly against force, and that, accordingly, commands and strong words should not be used. Also the Norwegians, of course, belonged to the Germanic brotherhood and, therefore, as far as was possible, should be treated on equal terms. This resulted in some Norwegians believing, at the beginning, that the Germans were not so terrible and dangerous as they expected. However, as time passed it became more and more difficult to keep up this pose.

Early in May the Gestapo confiscated the radio sets belonging to Norwegian Jews who had been living in the country for a long time. And, to show our feelings, we did not hoist the national flag on 17th May, the Norwegian Independence Day, which had been the greatest yearly festival of the country. The Germans, on the other hand, chose this day to show special films of their conquest of Norway. The students and the whole population rose in tumult, and they would not allow the shameless film to be shown anywhere that day. When Terboven, the Reichskommissar, was told of this tactless offence against our feelings, he simply could not understand that the Germans had done anything wrong. The pictures were genuine, he argued. Why not show it this day as well as any other day?

I had the opportunity of observing from close quarters what the Administrative Council really achieved up till the 25th September, when they were dismissed without any formalities by *Reichskommissar* Josef Terboven. During this half-year they had to solve the most difficult problems, not only financial, economic, social, and national problems, but everything concerning the occupation. Pressed by the Germans, besieged by Norwegians and opportunists who agitated for an arrangement with the Germans, they were always in a very difficult position. Since the troubled years of distress 1807–1814, no Norwegian institution has had such a responsible task.

At the beginning the Administrative Council only had to administer Oslo and a very few other districts, but as the invasion penetrated throughout Norway, more and more of the country came under their administration, and by the last days of May the greater part of Norway was occupied. The administration of the parts of Norway that came under the Administrative Council was performed by *Fylkes-Männer*—twenty higher administrative officials—in the country districts, and by the municipal authorities in the towns.

From the 21st April Hitler appointed Josef Terboven, a former bank clerk in the Rhineland, who had been made a Gauleiter in Krupps district in Essen, as *Reichskommissar* in Norway. The Reichskommissar exercises the supreme authority of government. He was assisted by his staff, the *Reichskommissariat,* which had taken over the Sterling building. This was divided into three main departments: administration, national economy, and propaganda. Then came the Senior Chief of the S.S. and Police of North (Nord), together with the commanders of the Civil Police (*Ordnungs-polizei*), and the Security Police (i.e. Gestapo), the latter having taken up residence in the Foreign Office.

The Reichskommissar had branches in various other places and also *Bezirkskommissars* (District Commissioners), and beyond this, further branches of the Security Police and the S.D. as well as the Civil Police and armed S.S.

From now on Norwegian administrative bodies, especially those concerned with finance, economics, production (price stabilizing), social welfare, and the police, became double-fronted. For not only the Administrative Council, and all forms of Norwegian administration, but also all the public organizations and the Bank of Norway, were forced to work together with the Reichskommissariat, who were desperately trying to gain a stranglehold on the political, economic and social life of Norway. Like an enormous octopus the Reichs-kommissariat uncurled its tentacles, and began to suck the life blood of the Norwegian people.

When on the 7th June the King and the Government had to leave the northern part of Norway, and the military operations in Norway ended in the withdrawal of the Allied forces from Narvik and the rest of Norway, the situation was again completely changed. The whole of Norway was now under German occupation and the Administrative Council in its existing form was not sufficient. On the 11th June representatives of the different Norwegian political parties presented a plan to transform the Administrative Council into a so-called *Riksräd*, a State Council, composed of the members of the Administrative Council widened by representatives of Labour and of Northern Norway. They were merely following the same ideas as that of the 15th April. They did not want to impair the power of the legal government which, being in England, was no longer able to function in Norway.

This plan, however, the Germans would not permit to be published, as they considered the time was now ripe to discuss the whole situation and to come to a decision about the King and the Government.

CHAPTER 3

The First Round

The request for the King's Abdication

1. The Ultimatum of 13th June

SUDDENLY, on the 13th June, the Germans made a counter-stroke. They presented an ultimatum to the Administrative Council, and then a terrible crisis arose. Many people, especially the Swedish Minister of Foreign Affairs, made a very great mistake in believing that the war was over after the evacuation of Norway. On the contrary. Only then did the real fight for the old kingdom of Norway, for our freedom and independence, for the soul of the people begin, this heroic spiritual fight without weapons, this terrible test of patience, endurance, and self-sacrifice, which is still going on. Now all real Norwegian men and women had to struggle every hour of the day for their conscience, and to defend everything they held sacred.

To understand why the Germans presented their ultimatum on the 13th June one must understand the methods of the Nazi war of nerves. It was from a psychological point of view that they chose this very moment of deepest depression to force us to surrender. At that time the Norwegian people felt terribly alone and abandoned. At the beginning most people believed in an early liberation, but very soon one disappointment followed another. The evacuation of Aandalsnes was followed by Namsos, and then came the terrible month of June, when everything on which we had built our hopes suddenly collapsed. We had believed in the power of the French army, and when German officers in Norway told us that they would smash France within three weeks, we did not believe it. But when the Dutch army surrendered, the Maginot Line was broken at Sedan and the Belgian army forced to surrender, then people in Norway began to believe in Hitler's time schedule. When German officers said, further, that they would be in London within three weeks, several people thought that unfortunately they must be right.

No one seemed capable of resisting them, and many of our people became depressed under the shadow of what seemed the inevitability of a final German victory. The defeat of France or, as we thought, the betrayal of France, was a crushing blow because our people loved and trusted France so deeply. Norwegians could not understand how Pétain could submit so abjectly, how such a great Empire as that of the French could capitulate while Poland, Norway, Holland, and Belgium, though reduced to a similar plight, were fighting on. It was widely felt that this could only mean that France had no confidence in the power of Great Britain, that France saw the Allied cause, including that of the British, as utterly and irretrievably lost. This being so, what could poor Norway think or do? It was not merely that Norwegians felt disappointment and bitterness towards the British and listened to people who asserted that Great Britain had left us in the lurch, that we had been let down, and so on, but they were also disappointed at the cold attitude of the Swedish Government, representing their nearest kinsfolk and neighbours. The King and the Government were far away, and the people at that time did not fully realize that it was Norway's good fortune that the State and Kingdom of Norway still existed abroad, and that our national flag was flying on our merchant fleet of 4,000,000 tons. Many, though perhaps not the majority of the people, were on the verge of despair, convinced that the only thing left to do was to make some sort of arrangement with the invaders. When, therefore, the Germans presented their ultimatum on the very same day as their entry into Paris, it was to impress the Norwegian leaders with the feeling that resistance was futile.

The German demands were as follows: The Storting, the Norwegian Parliament, should be convened in Eidsvoll, the most sacred place in our modern history, where the constitution of 1814 was born. There the members of the Parliament should repeal the Elverum decision of the Storting, to give the Government full powers, and then depose the King and the royal family and dismiss the Government. In their place there should be established a Norwegian State Council with authority in all internal questions, and with control of finance, economy, administration, police, and social and cultural life. The Administrative Council should be dissolved because, in reality, it represented the King's Government and was an emergency institution. The German Reichkommissar, Terboven, would be withdrawn and replaced by an 'Extraordinary Kommissar of the Fuehrer', but until such an appointment was made Terboven himself should perform these duties! Also the Swastika on the Storting building (Parliament House) would be lowered and the Norwegian flag hoisted again. The Germans also held out a prospect that the powers and scope of the German Civil Service and the Gestapo in Norway would be diminished.

If the Storting did not accept these demands, the Germans would establish a Government of Kommissars, and put Nazis into every branch of the Norwegian Administration and Institutions. The German negotiator, Delbrügge, declared that Norway, in this case, would never have any peace, and at the same time hinted at sending every young man liable for military service to the front, or into forced labour in Germany. This devilish scheme, which was never officially put forward or sanctioned by the German Commander-in-Chief in Norway, General von Falkenhorst, made a deep impression upon the members of the Presidential Board and other leading politicians. Like American Senators and Congressmen, and also I think, many members of the British Parliament, our politicians were mostly interested in local questions and the problems of their own constituencies. Very few of them had any knowledge of foreign policy or the broader aspect of national history. They did not know the Germans very well, and they were completely ignorant of Nazi mentality and methods. A few of them were born defeatists, others were temporarily weak and downhearted, some were also opportunists, but the majority did not understand what the

Nazi plan really was, and they hoped to protect the inner life
of Norway against Nazi infiltration, and save what they could
out of the wreckage. They did not understand that you
cannot trust the most solemn word or pledge of the Nazi;
that making and breaking pledges, for the Germans, is merely
a part of their policy and tactics. Unlike the English, the
Germans recognize nothing in the nature of a gentleman's
agreement. The English had, like others, made this mistake
of thinking a pact could be safely made with Hitler, and to
their great cost; Al Capone might well be jealous of the
German methods. Nobody could trust them. One might get
a result to-day, but they would surely break their bargain the
next week or later, and say that the situation was not the same.
This sad experience of many oppressed peoples was not
comprehended by many of our politicians and influential
citizens. They still did not understand what had really
happened. They refused to believe that the Germans would
nazify us and destroy our Norwegian way of life. They had
to undergo the same experience as Schuschnigg, Hacha, and
Colonel Beck. The negotiations horrified them, and opened
their eyes, and revealed to them the infernal immorality of
the Hitler mentality.

It must also be remembered that the Norwegian people
were completely ignorant of what was going on in Oslo during
the fateful days from the 13th to 18th June.

Quite by accident I managed to get hold of the German
Ultimatum of the 13th June, the day after it was issued. I
hurriedly got some copies made, and then made a great effort
to organize the resistance by gathering together as many
prominent people as I could get hold of, to try to persuade
them to exert their influence with the politicians. Even the
people in the capital, who were most vitally concerned, knew
nothing about the ultimatum until some days had elapsed
except what they had learned from their newspapers, the
editors of which had been forced to write articles against the
King and the Government. Those outside the capital knew
even less about this matter of historic importance. The text
of the Ultimatum has never been published, and what took

place during the days following its issue—the German and Norwegian counter-proposals—is known only to a few people. The great masses are still ignorant of the details of the negotiations, and know only of the main trends and the final result—which they learnt of through the broadcasts from London. The great majority of the Storting were not present in Oslo during these days of the negotiations, and public opinion was not represented because the public knew nothing. Very few people took part in these negotiations, and many of the members of the Parliament were not present until the last days. They were not informed of what had taken place before their arrival ; they were not even shown the various documents relating to these most vital questions, but were forced to make a decision in a hurry. In September, for instance, some of them were completely surprised when they discovered what had really taken place during this time. This was just a part of the German method: always to present an ultimatum with a few hours' time-limit, accompanied by violent threats and promises. Always a rush, always a hurry, so that people should not be able to think it over.

From now on, the Presidential Board of the Storting, consisting of six members (as President Hambro was in Great Britain, he was represented by a new member of his party), a committee concerned purely with technical details, and having no constitutional executive authority, took the lead in the negotiations, as the representatives of the Storting. The Presidential Board worked in conjunction with the Administrative Council—more especially with its Chairman, Mr. Christensen—with the elected representatives of the leading political parties, and with the Chairman of the Trades Union Congress. In the beginning they also consulted Mr. Berg, Chief Justice of the Supreme Court, and the Bishop of Oslo, Bishop Berggrav. At the outset they refused to depose the King and violate the Constitution. Under the leadership of the Supreme Court, whose members individually declared that the Storting had no executive rights, the above-mentioned politicians and representatives proposed that the Presidential Board should ask the Supreme Court to establish the State Council, under the leadership of the Chairman of the Administrative Council, Mr. Christensen, and then convene the Storting to sanction the action of the Presidential Board, and to decide on the extent of the power which should be invested in the State Council. They elected a committee, consisting of the Chief Justice, the Bishop of Oslo, and Mr. Harbech, a member of the Administrative Council, to negotiate with the Germans on the basis that the King and the Government should not be dismissed. Further than this the Supreme Court, as the guardian of the Constitution, would not go.

From the 15th April until December, when the Supreme Court resigned in protest against the abandonment of the rule of law in Norway, every member of the Supreme Court took a courageous attitude in defence of the great principle of our democracy, the first rule in the old Royal laws of the Sagas: 'The land shall be built on law.'

However, the Germans rejected the Norwegian proposal on the night of Saturday, 15th June, and from then on the Chief Justice and the Supreme Court took no more part in the negotiations, although they were still consulted on various questions and decisions. From now on only the Presidential Board and the Administrative Council, the elected representatives of the political parties, the Chairman of the Trades Union Congress, and the representatives of the Producers' Associations, took part in the negotiations. They had no constitutional authority to make any binding agreement for the people, though actually the Storting was now involved, but not committed, by what the Presidential Board signed.

During these gloomy days some of the members of the Parliament either accidentally, or in response to communications received from people who were on the spot, arrived in Oslo and took part in the negotiations; but they were not acting as a properly constituted body and they were only partly informed as to what was happening.

The big question now was whether the Presidential Board of the Storting, and the other negotiators, should continue the negotiations, or, without any further discussion, simply refuse the terms of the ultimatum which expired on Monday, the

17th, at 8 p.m. Already the Administrative Council was divided in its opinions. A strong minority still refused to go any further, but many people even now had not been able to make up their minds. I met many such people on Saturday, 15th June, and tried to convince them that they should make no more concessions. My impresssion was that the whole situation was in a state of flux, and that developments in the war situation in general would exert a tremendous influence upon the decisions that these wavering people would have to make. There were, of course, several opinions about what to do, but we could clearly distinguish two different points of view and modes of procedure.

2. For and Against

As I have said before, those who were still willing to negotiate were not traitors or even bad patriots. Many of them really believed that they were doing Norway a great service, and that they could spare our people from the most terrible trials. They acted as they did in good faith, to avoid, as they thought, the imposition of a German administration or a Quisling regime. They tentatively agreed to concessions which they believed would secure some sort of acceptable Norwegian administration. They argued as follows: the Germans have the power, and we have to adjust ourselves to this fact, and the changed conditions. We will fight for the King as long as we can—to quote the latin sentence: *ultra posse nemo obligatur*. They meant that if Great Britain won the war, the King and the Government would come back, but if the Germans won, it would be wise to have secured an arrangement with them beforehand, to avoid Norway's being placed in the position of a protectorate when the peace negotiations began.

Some of them were afraid that the people would not be able to stand up to real attempts at nazification, that there was a danger that our culture would be destroyed for a hundred years. They thought that the world would understand that we were forced to choose between life and death. To my surprise, some outstanding politicians lived under the false illusion that they really would be able to get a genuine Norwegian administration, and even obtain control of the press and broadcasting.

Those, however, who resisted the German demands at all costs maintained that we had already gone too far in concessions. The only thing we could do was to stand fast by the constitution and international law, and let the Germans violate them. The Germans respected only a firm attitude, and regarded any weakness as cowardice. In reality they despised the Quislings, as one of the German officers once said to one of them: 'Get out, you dirty rascal; you are neither Norwegian nor German.' Our first line of defence ought to be a legal one, because if we were once forced to break the law, we could never stop, and would go on slipping until we were completely demoralized. The Nazi plan was very clear. Their chief purpose was to break the morale of the Norwegians, to force us to violate the Constitution, to legalize what they erroneously called the revolution, and then to break every promise and nazify the country through Quisling, or someone else. They would dissolve the political parties in the same way as Hitler had done in Germany. As Terboven brutally explained to us on the 25th September,[1] the negotiations were chiefly an object lesson to show the people that the politicians and the democracies had nothing to die for. We could not obtain anything by a premature capitulation, except the destruction of our moral position in the world. If we surrendered before Germany had really won the war, the old kingdom of Norway would have ceased to exist. We would then have no King, no Government, no Legations, no national merchant fleet, and then Norway would really become a protectorate.

What could the Germans really offer us? They said: 'Coal, machinery, industrial products, etc.' But many of our experts said we could not expect very much, and later, their experience proved to be true. The so-called buying of Norwegian products was nothing but robbery. The Germans plundered

[1] For full text of Terboven's speech, see Appendix 4, p. 137.

us by paying in Norwegian money taken from the Bank of Norway, or in worthless German cheques. For example, they over-paid all the people who worked on their new aerodromes and fortifications. Some of them were paid from 20 to 40 kroner a day (more than £1 to £2), and in the beginning many of these people—some of them had hitherto been unemployed—did not understand that they were being bribed with their own money, drawn on the Bank of Norway. At the Gardermoen aerodrome, an Austrian soldier, who was in charge of the Norwegian workers, and listened to their satisfied comments on their high pay, said to them: 'We had the same experience in Austria. In the beginning the people were paid 20 Austrian shillings a day, after a while this dropped to 10 shillings, then to five, then to nothing—and so then to forced labour!'

We had never belonged to a German *Lebensraum* which for us would be a mortuary chamber. The decline of the old Norwegian Atlantic Empire began with the arrival of the Hanseatic League in the thirteenth century. We were a sea-faring country. From old times the ship was the symbol of Norway. Our *Lebensraum* is the sea, and the spirit of the sea filled us. Like the British we are children of liberty.

The Germans threatened to create a Government of Kommissars, as Delbrügge told us: 'You don't know what that means, they will rush at you like ferocious bulls.' To that the national opposition answered: 'Just try it, we don't think you can.' They had already discovered that the Achilles heel of the Germans was their bad civil administration. We were certainly impressed by their military machine and therefore we at first believed that their civil administration would be on the same level. The old imperial civil service had always been a model of efficiency, but our provincial governors, our civil service, and all those institutions which had to co-operate with the Germans every day, were at first surprised and then horrified when they saw the gulf that lay between the Nazi military and civil administrative organs, and later experience confirmed on a big scale their first impressions. One prominent Norwegian politician and administrator told the

Storting: 'Since I have seen the Germans at work with their New Order I am filled with admiration for our old Norwegian machine.' No words can describe this civil administration, as it showed itself in Norway, so inert was it in all its functions.

Under these circumstances we could never allow that the Storting, once called 'Norway's anchor in distress', should destroy the constitution of Eidsvoll.

The Germans might try to bribe the farmers by raising the prices, the worker by raising the wages. In a few cases they might succeed. In every country defeatists, opportunists, and political rats are to be found, but the people in themselves were sound. The choice was now a fatal one: now or never. If the leaders betrayed Norway, the people would go down. If we capitulated, our descendants in a similar situation would have to follow our example. But if we stood firm in these decisive moments of our history, the people would be steeled and our descendants would regard us as worthy of the 'Fathers of the Constitution of Eidsvoll'.

3. The Capitulation of the 18th June

But evil destiny overtook us. On the evening of the 15th June, we began to realize that the French army was completely broken. Therefore the negotiations continued on Sunday, the 16th, and the Presidential Board of the Storting and the other negotiators were driven from one redoubt to the other, under the pressure of German threats. Delbrügge reiterated his threat to put German Kommissars into power, 'but', he added, 'this will not be a permanent arrangement. Later we will put a Norwegian Government into power, but it will be a government which you will not be willing to see, and we will give it full liberty of propaganda.'

An opinion expressed by Dr. Delbrügge provides an excellent example of the Nazi way of thinking and of the gulf there is between the Norwegian and the German conception of life.

'I wish,' he said, 'that you would understand clearly that the Fuehrer is a friend of heroic conduct and has a generous attitude towards those people who show courage. If I, therefore, could tell him that it has been a great sacrifice for the Norwegian people to take the decision to depose the King and the Government, the Norwegians would, by this sacrifice, win from him something essential, which would be absolutely unobtainable if they waited until it became utterly unavoidable to take this decision. Remember this mentality of our Fuehrer. A closer union of the Germanic people is our aim. We must demand a certain heroism of those whom we shall deem our worthy associates ("Mitgänger").'

The Norwegians tried, as long as possible, to avoid deposing the King and dismissing the Government. Then on the 17th the great landslide came, when the hero of Verdun, Marshal Pétain, asked for an armistice. This black day in the brightest month of the year decided the course of the negotiations. It was a great setback and the negotiators were forced to give way to the German demands, but they still refused to depose the King. The ultimatum expired on Monday evening without any result, but during the night and the next morning the whole Presidential Board, and the leaders of the political parties, the Chairman of the Trades Union Congress, and Mr. Christensen, and three other members of the Administrative Council, capitulated. They agreed to send a formal request to King Haakon in London, asking for his abdication—and also for the resignation of the legal Government, which had left Norway with him. In case of refusal the Presidential Board promised to vote for the dethronement, but they refused to guarantee that the members of the Storting would do the same. The members of the Storting were still not committed.

But now came the great disappointment. The Presidential Board were certain that they would be permitted to explain to the King how it had all happened, and that the Supreme Court regarded all these measures as unconstitutional. They wrote to him an explanatory letter on 22nd June.[1] But the Germans said: 'No,' and the letter of 27th June [2] to the King

---

[1] For full text see Appendix 1, p. 127.
[2] For full text see Appendix 2, p. 129.

only contained the request without any commentary. They also believed that they would be able to decide on the form of Government, but the Germans interfered and demanded that instead of nine ministries we should have fifteen in the new State Council. This was the 'New Order'! As far as the members were concerned they interfered still more. They accepted four members of the Administrative Council, who were willing to continue, and a few other respectable persons, but they rejected most of the other Norwegian candidates. For instance, no prominent officials of the Labour movement were to be accepted, and only two members of the Labour party were admitted instead of the four or five members which the Germans had suggested. The Germans proposed instead pro-German Norwegians, even suspect persons of such an inferior capacity that they were the laughing stock of the country when it became known. Yet in spite of this, the majority of the new State Council was not pro-German.

And on one point they stood firm. They absolutely refused to accept any member of the Quisling party. The Germans tried to persuade them, but without any result. But then the devil appeared with all his temptations. This story is told here because it contains in a nutshell the Nazi tactics: if offered a finger the Nazis will certainly take the whole hand. They presented Axel Stang, a wealthy young countryman, insignificant, and without real influence, as a candidate, and said: 'If you take him we will promise you that Quisling shall leave Norway for the rest of the war, to visit the Channel ports and bombarded cities as our honoured guest.' The members of the Presidential Board thought this was an excellent bargain. 'We don't fear Mr. Stang,' they said, 'he cannot do much harm, but to get rid of Quisling is a great advantage for us.' And so they accepted and signed a secret agreement, whose contents were first revealed to the other Norwegian politicians in the autumn. They did not understand that they had sacrificed the most valuable principle and that the Nazis had got a foot into the inner citadel of Norway.

There are many signs that, during these negotiations, the different German groups finally disagreed, and it was a great mistake on the part of the Norwegian negotiators that they did not take advantage of this. Some of the Germans really wanted an agreement, but the aim of Terboven was solely to compromise the Storting, as he admitted in his big speech on 25th September.[1] However, Reichkommissar Terboven's weapon proved to be a boomerang, which came back and hit him. The negotiations were, for the Norwegian people, an unparalleled lesson in Nazi trickery and deceit.

About the 1st July, all the sixteen members of the State Council were selected by the Presidential Board, Mr. Christensen, Delbrügge and the German Reichskommissariat. Already on the 24th of June, Delbrügge had informed them that Hitler had declared his satisfaction with the agreement. The next thing to do was to convene the Storting to depose the King, dismiss the government, and then establish the State Council. But then for weeks nothing happened. Before, the Nazis had always been in a hurry. But now nothing happened. The members of the Storting were asked to be ready for a meeting on the 15th July, but nothing happened. Whenever I happened to meet members of the Administrative Council—which was still the only functioning central administrative body—they asked me: 'Do you know anything about what's going to happen?' I said: 'No, but you certainly must know something.' They shook their heads. Under the completely unstable conditions then existing, it was impossible for them to come to any decision. For example, they had to prepare the budget, but they did not even know whether they would be dismissed the following day or not. Nobody knew anything. The Germans said: 'Wait until Hitler has made his speech.' Hitler made his speech, but nothing happened. 'We must first hear the British answer,' said the Germans, but when Lord Halifax replied, still nothing happened. It is difficult to account for this strange inactivity. Was it that the different groups of Nazis were disagreeing; that they were beginning to understand that they had made a terrible blunder, as their civil police all over the country were constantly informing

[1] See Appendix 4.

them that they had?. Or was it due to the whims of Quisling,
who was now in Berlin and in contact with Rosenberg and
Hitler himself? I cannot give an answer, but in these days
when nothing seemed to happen, the really great thing
happened: the Norwegian people rose in defence of their
King and Constitution, and found themselves.

4. The Revolt of the Norwegian People

The Germans had missed their opportunity. In June and
July they had a chance of coming to an arrangement with us,
if they had behaved decently, by playing on the sore theme
that we had been let down and abandoned. But they went
about it in the wrong way. They could not resist or delay
their impulse to assail our King when he had come nearer
than ever before to the heart of the Norwegian people. Here
the Germans made their terrible mistake, their great psychological blunder. They showed themselves masters of false
psychology, unable to understand that to ask the Storting and
the people, especially at that time, to remove the King, was
to wound deeply the most sacred feeling of the Norwegian
people. Before the war, the King had been very popular, but
when he was being hunted and bombed during the war the
love of the people for King Haakon grew and grew, and after
the attempted deposition, King Haakon became our 'Saga
King', a symbol of the Constitution, the liberty, the living
history of all that Norway stands for and still fights for. It was
a wonderful feeling that swept through Norway. In a few
days there was a great revival, a mighty reaction in spirit
against the insolent German demand for the abdication of the
King, and it spread like wildfire throughout the country. The
common people: the sailors, the fishermen, the peasants, and
the small farmers, labour, the students and intellectuals,
people of every class and rank refused to depose their King
and instead rallied around him more strongly than ever
before. Since that time this spirit has daily been gaining in
strength. It took some time before the people in Norway got
to know what had really happened, but when the essential

facts were made known, by means of printed and duplicated leaflets, and news sheets circulating all over Norway, broadcasts from London, and leading articles in the provincial press, which had managed to evade the German censorship, public opinion rapidly formed itself and grew in strength. For many it was not merely a political, but also a religious question. The soul of Norway was at stake. You could often hear simple people imperfectly quote this passage from the Scriptures: 'Better to lose your life than your soul.'

Members of the Storting were bombarded with letters, urging them not to give way. Everywhere people produced small flags and portraits of the King. People in all walks of life were furious. One member of the Storting said to me as early as July: 'My choice is easy. Either my constituents or the Germans would surely shoot me—and I prefer the German bullet.' The German Commandant at Geilo, said to a young Norwegian diplomat: 'You will have to give in. Remember the German army is mighty.' My friend answered: 'But God is mightier.' On the 8th July the King, in a radio broadcast from London, gave his answer to the Presidential Board and declared: 'The freedom and independence of the Norwegian people is to me the first commandment of our Constitution, and I feel that I follow this commandment and best serve the interests of the Norwegian people in holding fast by the position and the task a free people gave me in 1905.'[1] The Norwegians were listening in every house in the utmost anxiety of mind, filled with anger and sorrow to learn of the request made to the King by the Presidential Board, and were relieved and proud to hear the King's refusal to abdicate. But in the newspapers the King's reply was cut down to a few lines by the censor. This blunder and falsification only strengthened our feelings and our contempt for the Nazi mentality. So spontaneous and strong was the spirit of resistance that, as early as the 17th July, one of the Presidents of the Storting wrote a letter to Delbrügge in which he stated that the people were so opposed to the dethronement of the King that the Storting would never agree to the German

[1] For full text see Appendix 3, p. 132.

demand, and he asked him, therefore, to reconsider the matter.

Externally the revival was not uniform throughout our far-flung country, but everywhere the feeling was intense, especially along the western coast, where it is seen and felt most keenly that Norway is at war.

In Bergen the people shouted 'Hurrah' in the streets, when they saw the Royal Air Force in the sky.

In Stavanger the inhabitants became furious when the Germans transformed a well-known chapel into an ale house.

CHAPTER 4

Norway Finds Herself

1. On the West Coast

WHEN I went from Oslo to the mountains in July, I did not like the spirit in the capital. Everything seemed to be affected by the Nazis. You could never avoid the German soldiers, marching and singing in the streets: '*Wir fahren, wir fahren gegen England.*' Everywhere you could see them eating chocolate spread with butter, or ordering nine fried eggs at a time. To impress us, they often arranged tank-parades in the main street. You had the feeling that you had lice on your body. Many people said: 'What can we do? We must come to an arrangement, we must have things working again.'

I was pleasantly surprised to find not only fresh air, but also fresher minds in the mountains. Ordinary folk were still confident. Everybody tried to listen to the broadcasts from London, even old women went to bed early in the evening so as to wake up at one o'clock in the night. In one little parish in the mountains there was only one radio set. In this house everybody assembled every afternoon. Oslo broadcasts were believed by nobody.

On the southern coast the spirit was even better. The Germans helped the growing optimism by their unimpressive attempts at embarking for the invasion of England, and the view took root that the Germans in Norway, on the whole, were sick of their invasion plans. We gained the firm impression that German soldiers in Norway feared the turbulent waves of England.

I witnessed some of these attempts, or exercises, elaborate in preparation and with a considerable number of horses as well as men. Many of these soldiers came from the interior of Germany and, being unable to swim, looked more than a little ridiculous as invaders.

At Stavanger, one of the great embarkation ports for invasion, the following incident occurred during the last days of August:—

One hundred and fifty German officers took a pleasure trip on a steamer in the beautiful fjords near Stavanger. They had plenty to drink and became very merry, and to amuse themselves they started firing at some empty bottles in the water with machine-guns, but they manœuvred the steamer so badly that they finished by destroying some of the wooden landing quays. On returning to the entrance of the harbour they steamed up the wrong side of the buoys, with the result that the ship capsized, and forty of the potential invaders of Great Britain were drowned, only twenty-five yards from the shore.

The invasion attempts were undoubtedly marred by mutinies here and there, for the soldiers soon objected to being crowded into the holds of fishing craft, covered over with nets and wire netting, just like pigs in a cart going in to market, and then being taken for trips on the restless sea. This huddled live freight became sick time after time, no matter how often the experiments were repeated, and the smaller fishing craft had to be abandoned as unsuitable for invasion purposes. Some of the mutineers were shot, others were transported to Oslo where, during the night, they were observed marching—two or three hundred of them, with their hands tied behind their backs—to their unknown fate. I could get no confirmation about the mutinies which were reported to have taken place in Bergen, but fishermen on the coast near Bergen told of how they had found the dead bodies of German soldiers—two or three of them chained together, with their hands tied behind their backs—floating in the sea.

Whether the whole idea of an invasion expedition from Norway has been given up or not cannot be said, but it would certainly be of a very different nature in 1941 to that of 1940.

On the coast much more was happening to stimulate the Norwegians. German ships were being sunk by torpedoes or mines, which for military reasons were never reported from Britain, so the people in this part of the country realized much more fully the fact that Norway was at war. In Arendal, for instance, which in days long past was the centre of the Norwegian sailing fleet but to-day is only a very quiet town, the German commander of the garrison decreed that when the flag bearing the swastika was lowered every evening, in the centre of the harbour, all Norwegians who were passing at that time were to salute it. If they did not do so they were to be arrested. This decree, and all the arrests which followed, did not improve the relations between the invaders and the Norwegians.

2. The Press

The ordinary people still trusted England: 'The British are moving terribly slowly,' they said, 'but they will win in the end.' Outside Oslo the newspapers dared to write more freely, because at the beginning they were only censored by the military. I could quote many good stories from these papers. When Bergen, on 16th June, was bombed by the Royal Air Force, and many houses were hit by the German anti-aircraft guns, the German censor presented seven different headlines, all insulting the King, and our newspapers had to pick out one of them. The headlines from which they had to choose were as follows:—

(1) Did King Haakon know that his British friends bombarded Bergen?

(2) The King sent us help from England.

(3) Royal greetings from England: bombs over Bergen.

(4) Cordial thanks, King Haakon, Bergen is burning.

(5) Did King Haakon, in London, know that Bergen was burning?

(6) As soon as the King arrived in London our Norwegian citizens were bombarded to death.

(7) King Haakon continues the war. Bergen is his first victim.

One paper on the western coast, however, published all seven headlines at the same time, to the fury of the Germans. Another editor, a former sea captain, published the secret instructions from the Germans to the press, about what they were allowed to write or not to write. Every number of his paper contained the most daring articles, and it gained many subscribers in the capital, until it was stopped and the editor was arrested in August. For instance, on 12th July he printed a full length photograph of Quisling; under the photograph he printed a verse from a famous old seventeenth century folk song—applying the meaning of it to Quisling. The literal translation of the verse, which in Norwegian is rhymed, is as follows: 'Woe to each Norwegian who cannot burn with anger every time he has to look upon this man!' The Gestapo immediately ordered the editor to Bergen, but he replied that he could not come unless his travelling expenses were paid. After this nothing further happened, and he continued to publish the wittiest and most amusing stories, well-known verses—between the lines of which Norwegians could read his real meaning and opinions—and many patriotic articles. Then, suddenly, he was stopped, but his editorial staff of one did not lose courage and tried to continue with the paper under a new name. However, he did not succeed. I happened to pay the editor a visit to congratulate him; on the same day he was arrested. The day before I had paid a similar visit to an editor—a woman—in a neighbouring town. Her paper had been stopped the day before my visit, because she had written the most patriotic leading articles about our ancient traditions, and stated that by courage and loyalty to our old ideals we would survive the catastrophe. She was still very proud that she had written these articles, even after she and her children had lost their means of livelihood. 'It is much better,' she said to me, 'to sink with the Norwegian flag flying than to make for an enemy harbour.' A few days later she was arrested and taken to Oslo.

In Oslo the censorship was much more strict. The German censor had no understanding of Norwegian cultural life—he had never heard of Fridtjof Nansen, nor had the chief of the Gestapo, Dr. Felix. He did not understand our mentality and perpetrated the most ridiculous blunders. For instance, when the official paper of the Labour party published a little article in *Petit* about the German soldiers incessantly humming '*Wir fahren, wir fahren*, etc.' the paper was prohibited and the editor put into prison. The first victim of the German censor was the Oslo radical paper *Dagbladet*, which was given eight days' notice that from 29th May it would be censored before publication. This made it extremely difficult to get the paper ready in time, because very often the censor deleted a whole page. When, on 14th June, the editor tried to avoid the censor, and refused to write against the King and the legal Government, the paper was banned for an indefinite period. When it appeared in circulation again, eight weeks later, there was a new chief editor, and it had much more the appearance of a Nazi paper. The Salvation Army paper, *Krigsropet* (War Cry), was one of the few papers which dared to write a long article in honour of the King on his birthday, 3rd August. The editor was immediately arrested and put into prison for a month and the paper banned for half a year. Some other papers in the outlying districts of Oslo also contained articles, and many of them contained just a small notice which the local censorship did not discover.

During the first months of the German occupation, the Norwegian people did not understand that journalists and editors were forced, at the point of a revolver, to write insulting articles which were revolting to the general public. Neither were they able, therefore, to appreciate the remarkable efforts which these same journalists and editors made to avoid publishing Nazi propaganda. Many papers daily received hundreds of letters from readers, cancelling their subscriptions. All the pictures in the papers had to be censored, and when Terboven made his speech outside the royal palace, in the beginning of June, the Norwegian papers were not allowed to print their own photographs but only those which were sent to them by the German censor.

On 17th May, the National Day of Norway, which was always celebrated all over Norway by flag parades and children's parades—in Oslo thirty to forty thousand white clad children would march through the streets to salute the King and the Royal Family—during the afternoon public speeches were made everywhere in commemoration of the great day. On that day, *Tidens Tegn*, one of the leading papers in Oslo, printed a famous speech of Dr. Fridtjof Nansen, which he had made in 1915 on the 17th May, and also a snapshot of the Royal Family and the Crown Prince and Princess, taken in 1939 on their return from their great tour in the United States. The German censor was furious. The editor was sent for and informed that his action constituted a very serious demonstration against German authority. The censor did not like the speech of Dr. Nansen because every word of it expressed a spirit which the Germans were now trying to suppress, but the worst thing, he said, was the photograph of 'the long man' (as he called the King). The best thing to do would be to stop the paper for ever. The editor replied that he could not understand why the censor was so angry. A few days before all editors had been informed that they could write about the 17th May, so long as they did so as usual and did not make use of it to demonstrate against the German army. The editor then explained that he had fully conformed to this order. The two main events of the day in Oslo were always the children's parade before the King, and the afternoon speeches—and these were excellent reasons for the photograph and the speech of Dr. Nansen! The censor let the editor go with a warning, but a short time after he was again disatisfied with him!

In many papers the editorial staff tried to give expression to their true feelings and opinions in the form of witticisms and humorous articles, which were generally not understood by the German censors until their attention was drawn to them by Quislings.

The following mackerel story, which is true, illustrates more of the German mentality than a long treatise. When the German cruiser *Blücher* was sunk in the Oslo fjord, inside Dröbak, we said to ourselves: 'Now we shan't be able to eat the famous Dröbak cod for some time, and we shan't be able to eat the mackerel at all, because it has something else to do.' In *Tidens Tegn*, a popular fictitious figure called 'Andriksen the harpist' used to write a few words of wisdom every day (they are difficult to translate because in Norwegian they are in rhymed verses). One day he wrote the following: 'Why take this round about way through the mackerel?' The Germans did not understand this insult. A few days afterwards Andriksen wrote: 'Eat mackerel all the same.' Then the censor called the editor into his office and told him that his paper would have to be censored beforehand every day, and that the word 'mackerel' from now on was forbidden in the paper. A few days afterwards the paper's weekly household recipe contained two mackerel dishes—the censor deleted both of them.

As early as June very detailed instructions had been given to the editors of all the papers about what to write, what not to write, and how to write. These instructions are typical of the German mentality, and some of the most significant ought to be quoted.

For example, official war communiqués from those countries with whom Germany is at war should not be published unless received direct from the Nazi-controlled Norwegian News Agency. News picked up from radio stations from countries at war with Germany must not be published.

The Nygaardsvold Government must not be defended. Speeches made by persons of the Royal Family, Government, or the General Staff, must not be printed, and pictures of these persons must not be published.

In foreign policy the German attitude must be respected, and countries which have entered into pacts with Germany must not be attacked.

News about the economic and financial situation which might create uneasiness must be carefully handled.

Nothing must be published which might create bad feeling between the German troops and the Norwegian population.

The communiqués from the German High Command must be prominently printed. The words 'world war' must not be used.

Editors who do not strictly adhere to these instructions will not only risk having their papers forbidden, but will also suffer personal consequences.

No profession in Norway has a greater percentage of arrested people than the journalistic one.

3. Growing Resistance in Oslo

When I returned to Oslo in August I was again surprised to find a new spirit of optimism growing there. Our people were beginning to understand clearly what was happening as they saw the Germans consistently breaking both their pledges and our laws. They saw Norway becoming what it is to-day— a country entirely without law, where no one is safe from arrest and imprisonment. A friend of mine, Mr. Oftedal, one of our most outstanding journalists, was not willing to write articles dictated by the Germans and resigned from the editorship of the paper *Stavanger Aftenblad* which his grand-father and father had founded, and tried to make his living as a teacher. Early in August he suddenly disappeared. His brother, a well-known physician, went to Oslo to ask the members of the Administrative Council if they could find out where he was, and a month later, they discovered that he was in a concentration camp near Bergen. In February, 1941, he was sentenced to death for espionage. His brother was later, together with two other prominent citizens of Stavanger, taken as a hostage to Oslo, as a reprisal for sabotage which had taken place in Stavanger.

Our people now found that prominent people were disappearing without leaving any traces, until later information reported them to be in gaol. They were editors, journalists, members of the Labour party, supporters of the Government returning from the war, persons distributing leaflets (the King's speeches and other documents), very outspoken people, boys cutting hair off the heads of girls who fraternized with German soldiers, even conservative members of the parliament, shipowners, etc. Nobody dared to speak aloud in the street as they had been accustomed to do, for as soon as two Norwegians started talking together, a third person would sneak up behind them and listen. A well-known journalist, belonging to the Oxford Group, was standing outside the

Telegraph Office in Oslo, talking to a friend. While they were talking a German lorry drew up, a soldier got out and came towards them. The journalist whispered to his friend: 'Don't say anything.' The soldier then came up and asked the journalist the way, but received no answer. Then the German said: 'Does this mean you will not answer?' 'Certainly,' replied the journalist. He was then immediately placed under arrest, but as the German went to take hold of his arm the journalist brushed his hand away, and the German became more and more furious. The journalist was imprisoned for over a month, and before being released he was asked to sign a declaration that he would not take any further part in the Oxford Group meetings. He refused. Finally the Germans gave up the attempt to force him to do this, and were satisfied that he had been forced to sign a declaration that he would not take part in any political propaganda. The telephone was constantly being tapped. Spies and informers were everywhere, especially the Quislings.

Our citizens felt German interference in every aspect of daily life, in the broadcasting, the telegraph agency, the press and the theatre, in politics and even in social life. Freemason Lodges, Rotary Clubs, for example, were dissolved, along with Women's Associations and Students' Societies. Old ladies belonging to the Oxford Group Movement were even under suspicion. The Nazis demanded that the members of the Shipowners' Association should make a speech to their captains at sea, calling them back to neutral ports, but the shipowners refused. They confiscated the property of the members of the Government, and Mrs. Koht, the wife of the Minister of Foreign Affairs, on returning from an outing with her two small grandchildren, discovered that she had to leave her house within half an hour. The leader of the Gestapo even dared to threaten this distinguished, charming lady. 'If you dare,' he said on the threshold of the house, 'to circulate false rumours and say that your house has been seized, you will be severely punished.' Mrs. Koht replied calmly: 'I never circulate false rumours, but this house is commandeered.'

The German Reichskommissar, Terboven, first decided to

move into the Royal summer residence at Bygdö, in spite of the promise given by the German Minister, Bräuer, a few days after the invasion, that the property belonging to the King would be respected, but he soon found that this was not good enough for him, and then moved to the beautiful residence of Crown Prince Olav, at Skougum, about ten miles from Oslo, which had recently been constructed and was equipped with all modern conveniences. Even so it did not satisfy Herr Terboven, and he started rebuilding and refurnishing the house. In the autumn the Germans also seized the King's winter house near Oslo.

Shortly after the Germans occupied Oslo they bought up all the fishing rods in the shops, and the officers boasted: 'This year we shall fish for salmon, and not the British.' However, as most of them didn't know anything at all about fishing, they cut a very ridiculous figure when they tried to imitate British habits. Near Skougum there is a lake called Semsvand, but we had never heard that there were any trout or salmon in it. However, one Sunday the farmers and people living near Skougum were amazed to see some of the members of Terboven's staff setting out from Skougum in plus fours and sport's dress, with their new fishing rods in their hands, to try their luck in the Semsvand! At least the invasion had provided a good laugh, for many days, for the inhabitants of this part of Norway.

These examples could be multiplied without end, but what would be the use? One has to experience such things at first hand, and day after day, before one can fully grasp what true Nazi behaviour is, even in a Nordic country. The Germans long ago proclaimed themselves a Nordic people, yet their aim is to destroy the real Nordic people. The realization of what the Nazis intend to do in Norway crept upon us slowly like a plague.

It had become clear, too, that the Germans were plundering our country on a terrible scale. Up till March 1st they had taken 1,700,000,000 Norwegian crowns from the Bank of Norway, and in one week sixty million crowns. This amount is increased by 150 million crowns every month. And we have had to pay more and more taxes. The newspapers had to explain that this was the fault of the old Government, now hiding in England, but our people preferred the explanation given in the broadcast from London that it was due to the expenses of the German occupation. Prices were rising and the wages, on the other hand, were cut down. The German soldiers were visibly becoming fatter and fatter. One article after another disappeared from the market. First eggs, then chocolate, rice, fat, and now meat and all the best fish. The Germans took the best vegetables. One day in August a German went into one of the largest grocers in Oslo and asked for fifty kilos of lard. The assistant told him he could only have one kilo. The German furiously reiterated his demand, but the assistant repeated that he was not allowed to supply one person with more than one kilo of lard. The German then left the store in a rage, and after a while he returned and requisitioned all the fats in the store.

There was, however, still no real food shortage in Norway, because the Norwegian Government before the war had bought great stores of provisions. The stores of clothing were rifled and the rest was rationed. Only then did the housewives become angry, understanding at last what so-called 'protection' by the Germans really meant. The following incident is an example of the reaction of the food queues to the German regime in Oslo. My wife was standing in a queue one day, with many other housewives who were talking and complaining about the soaring prices, when one woman exclaimed: 'Oh, this is good, this is wonderful. We shall be hungry, we shall freeze. I am glad, yes, glad, for it is the only way in which we shall all come to realize that we have the Germans here.'

Everything the Germans did had just the opposite effect to what they expected. When, in August, they sentenced three prominent Norwegians to death, people were not at all frightened, but became more and more furious, and we were proud when the condemned men refused to ask for pardon. During the September negotiations the Germans used these men as hostages, and threatened that their execution would be carried out if the members of the Storting did not surrender to the German demands. In the late autumn they were pardoned by the Fuehrer but it is said that they were sent to camps or prisons in Germany. The Germans seized the Institute of the Merchants' Association, situated in the main street of Oslo, and called it the *Deutsches Haus*. From the balcony hung an enormous Swastika, so huge that it almost obliterated the view of the Royal Palace. This flag reminded us every day of what we had lost.

There had been no hatred for the Germans before the 9th April, and this feeling did not become general all at once. We had been, in the main, distinctly pro-British and felt keen disappointment that the Royal Navy did not manage to stop the German invasion. But now the whole people hate and despise, not individual Germans, but the whole Nazi idea and the men sent to put it into practice. At the same time, we have become more and more optimistic. We were impressed by the fact that England was standing firm, and the hopes of most people began presently to turn towards this country, and by and by developed into a belief in a coming British victory. For the first time, the German schedule had gone wrong. The Germans had boasted that they would be in England in July, then in August, and then again they had to shift the date on to September.

Winston Churchill's inspiring speeches had a tremendous effect, the battle of Oran showed us that Great Britain was determined to fight to the death, and the great battle in the air for London, in September, destroyed for ever the most dangerous weapon of the fifth columnists in every country, the story that England was fighting to the last Norwegian and Frenchman. Reliable reports told about mutinies amongst the German soldiers at different places. In July they sang: '*Wir fahren, wir fahren*' exultantly; after the 15th September, they looked downhearted. Now the Norwegians have started to call the song the '*Niegelungenlied*'. And in Oslo we were again longing for bombing. I remember quite well a Saturday in the beginning of September, when I was working in the library of the University. Suddenly, at one o'clock, an air raid warning sounded, and hundreds of people ran into the shelters, full of joy and expectation. After only a few minutes the 'All Clear' was sounded. Never in my life have I heard so many curses at once; the people were bitterly disappointed. The British are too human, they said, they do not want to destroy our houses, but we will take the risk if only they can get a hit at the Germans.

Our greatest reserve of force, compared with the Germans, was our sense of humour and of the ridiculous side of the Nazi. Even under aggression we could still laugh, and many amusing incidents occurred. One day a Nazi came into the biggest warehouse in Oslo and made the Hitler salute: 'Heil Hitler! Where is the gentlemen's department?' The shopgirl answered quickly: 'God save the King, first turning to the left.' In April the Germans telephoned to a churchwarden in Oslo asking him if he had room for some hundred Germans, to which he replied: 'Certainly, we can find room for all of you in the churchyard.' The Nazis requisitioned the shop window of a tourist agency in the main street in Oslo, and adorned it with a life-size photograph of Adolf Hitler. Below it was written, in big letters: 'But you don't know him as he really is.' The window was guarded by three policemen, and Gestapo men mixed with the public to listen to what they said. One day a business man adorned his window with a picture of another house painter, the so-called 'House painter, Mr. Bjerke'. This pictorial advertisement of the biggest colour firm in Norway, Alf Bjerke, was extremely popular, and you could see this funny face all over the country. In this case, the business man put the following inscription beneath the picture: 'But this one you know.' The effect of the German exhibition was completely destroyed. Everybody laughed, and when they passed the photograph of Hitler they sneered at him saying: 'Oh, there is Mr. Bjerke's house painter.' (See illustration on page 49.)

Another friend of mine, a lady doctor, met some German soldiers one day and they asked her the way. She said to them in English: 'Do you mind if I answer in English?' When they had agreed to this she said: 'I don't know,' and left them!

On another occasion a Norwegian actress was sitting alone in a restaurant, having a cup of coffee. There were some empty chairs at her table and suddenly a German officer came up to her and asked if he could take a seat. She did not reply and the officer repeated his request, without any result. Then a Norwegian, perhaps a Quisling, sitting near her, said: 'Don't you understand what he says?' To which she replied: 'I cannot see why he should ask me if he may take a seat when they have taken the whole country!'

Another well-known actress was invited by Terboven to a reception at Skogum. She declined the invitation, giving as her reason that she never accepted an invitation when the host and hostess were absent!

Every day new stories were told or fabricated. When the German reverses in the air battle over London became known, people said: 'Have you heard the latest news?—Hitler has bought the finest radio set in the world.' 'Why?' 'That's the only way he can get London!'

After the Germans had lost so many ships in the fight for Norway, and especially after the loss of the cruiser *Blücher*, which was sunk by the torpedo batteries, any Norwegian soldiers taken prisoner used to tease the Germans by saying to them: 'Do you know that Hitler now wears a diving suit?' 'Why?' asked the German, surprised. 'To inspect his fleet,' they replied!

During the early autumn, the spirit of the national opposition was finding expression in the most remarkable ways in the Norwegian theatres. The actors said the most insulting things against 'our guests', in the most elegant manner, and the public roared with laughter.

In the summer the National Theatre had played the *Merry Widow*, and the theatre was booked up days before every performance. The play had been altered and every line turned against the Germans.

In another theatre a famous actor was playing in a parody of Ibsen's *Peer Gynt*, directed against the Germans. The allusion in the words: 'The winter may pass, and the spring go by, and the summer too, yes, the whole year may fly, but one day they will be gone,' were obvious to every Norwegian in the theatre, and people rocked with laughter. The Germans did not understand a word, so the young Quislings were brought in as informers and all the witticisms and allusions were deleted.

In a few weeks the whole situation had been changed. Every day the resistance was stiffening and the conviction was growing that, above all, we must remain loyal to our traditions of freedom, liberty, and decency.

Many of the people, who in the beginning had believed this war to be only a struggle between Germany and Great Britain, now became aware that Norway was not fighting for Great Britain, but for herself and for all that she held most precious in life.

Mr. Bjerke's "House Painter" makes one of his frequent appearances, this time in an advertisement for a well-known Norwegian paint. (See page 47.)

CHAPTER 5

The Second Round

The Negotiations and the Blitzkrieg on London.   The Rupture

THEN things began to happen again. It now became evident that the agreement between the Presidential Board and the Nazis regarding Quisling was a failure. Instead of having got rid of him, he was at present in Germany, trying to get rid of them. On Saturday, the 17th August, Quisling had an audience with the Führer, who now probably ordered him to return to Norway and try to form an administration on a broader basis. We do not know exactly what happened, but in any case it was a decisive meeting. For the German Nazi leaders in Norway, who really could know what value to put upon the influence of Quisling in Norway, this sudden decision was a disappointment. Terboven flew the next day to Berlin, as we were told, to try to advise Hitler against Quisling. General von Falkenhorst is also said to have been against him, and the negotiator, *Regierungspräsident* Delbrügge, openly said: 'I have been disowned,' and soon after left the country.

To understand the situation in Norway it must be remembered that the prestige of Hitler is linked with the position of Quisling. Quisling returned on the 20th and tried to get support from Labour and influential persons. At the same time he summoned to Oslo his so-called *Hird* or Storm-troopers, several hundred silly-looking young people, either to frighten us into submission or perhaps to try to obtain forcible possession of Norway by surprise. The Administrative Council ordered the head of the police in Oslo to send in armed police to defend the various government buildings in Oslo, but nothing happened. One day during this time I happened to see some Hird troops marching down the main street of Oslo to lay flowers before the monument of Henrik Ibsen. It was a very sad sight to watch these pitiful creatures, who had taken the magnificent name of Hird from the old Sagas. One of the onlookers turned to me and said: 'They look like idiot children.'

Twice in a few months Quisling had openly betrayed Norway in conspiracy with Adolf Hitler himself. Both in April and in August his own people had flatly rejected him, and even the German Command had no opinion of him. Now he could only obtain power by means of German bayonets and the Gestapo.

Nearly three months had passed since the German ultimatum in June, and our leading politicians still lived in suspense and ignorance of what was going to happen. All the different political parties together with the Trades Union Congress, the Employees' Associations and Producers' Associations now tried to form a common front on the 23rd August, but Terboven forbade this on the 26th and did not even permit them to publish their decision and declaration.

Suddenly, at one o'clock p.m. on Saturday, the 7th September, the Presidential Board was informed by Delbrügge that the negotiations were to be resumed at five o'clock that same afternoon. It was just like a stroke of lightning. One cannot expect people to be ready for negotiations on a Saturday at one o'clock, so the German procedure was in any case very extraordinary. Looking back it is very easy to explain this unusual date. It was not an ordinary Saturday, it was the Black Saturday, 7th September, when the *Blitzkrieg* struck London. Just as in June, the Germans chose the moment for presenting their ultimatum at a time when they were trying to strike the deathblow against their arch-enemy. The movements in June and September were analogous. They planned to crush the spirit of resistance of England and to wipe out the soul of the Norwegian people at the same time.

The Presidential Board of the Storting, the Administrative Council, and the other negotiators were informed at five o'clock on the same day that the Germans insisted upon their June demands. The Storting must now depose the King and dismiss the Government. The only new thing in their demands was that they went back on their earlier promises:—

(1) Reichkommisssar Terboven was to stay in Norway until the end of the war and would not be withdrawn as promised.

(2) The promise that Quisling should leave Norway was repealed.

(3) The flag ceremony at the Stortings building, which they had represented as a symbol of restitution, was not to take place.

(4) Instead of one Nasjonal Samling member in the State Council, they demanded three, with the result that two other strongly pro-German but anti-Quisling candidates had to be removed from the list which in July had been accepted as final.

The Germans had not only broken every pledge they had given, but also ignored the definite pre-supposition which should have formed the basis for the negotiations, that the Germans should give a written guarantee assuring the State Council an independent position as the real leader of Norway's administration. Without that there was no possibility of the Storting accepting the State Council. But instead of the definite guarantee from the German Reichskommissar they only received vague assurances from a subordinate, Delbrügge, who had already been let down by Hitler. Dr. Delbrügge declared as his interpretation, that he could not imagine anything but . . . he believed . . . he would give his attention to . . . he did not doubt . . . etc.

If the Storting did not accept this, he said, the Germans would at once put into operation a Government of Kommissars or a Quisling regime. In the end Delbrügge declared that both the Fuehrer and the Reichskommissar really preferred the former alternative, but we now had to understand that any permanent settlement of the future in the 'Nordic *Raum*' would depend upon collaboration. This was nothing but fraud and deceit. It was already quite clear to the majority that the Germans would only use the negotiations to compromise the Storting and the democratic parties, and that the Quisling regime had already been decided upon. In his long speech of the 25th September, which, as I have already said, was just one series of lies, Terboven declared that Quisling's party, Nasjonal Samling, had not interfered during these negotiations, but had been standing at ease the whole time. This story is completely untrue. Quisling and his followers had steadily increased their efforts to exert an influence on the negotiations—far from standing at ease, they had been standing with their rifles at the ready, prepared to fire at their own countrymen.

The hour of decision was at hand. The Germans demanded that the Presidential Board should summon all the members of the Parliament that very Saturday evening by telegram. They were to meet in Oslo on Monday morning, not in parliamentary session, but only in separate party meetings. The decisions would only be preliminary. If there really was a qualified majority (two-thirds) in favour of the terms of the German ultimatum, the Storting would be convened in full session to depose the King. Also on this point Terboven lied intentionally when he said that it was not necessary to have a two-thirds majority in the voting, although it is an established fact that Dr. Delbrügge had demanded this majority in his ultimatum.

As usual, the Germans tried to push through their demands in a hurry. The members of the Presidential Board answered that it was impossible for the members of the Storting to reach Oslo as early as Monday morning, and they proposed adjournment till Friday (in fact the members from the northern part of Norway did not arrive before Thursday). But the Germans refused. As the Presidential Board still insisted, the Germans granted a postponement till Tuesday only, because on Wednesday morning Terboven was to fly to the Fuehrer with the result. As in June, the general public were not informed that the different political parties of the Storting had been summoned to Oslo, but after a few days, of course, rumours had spread throughout the country, which was awaiting the result of the negotiations in a state of utmost tension. Since all the 150 members of the Storting had been summoned to Oslo, naturally more people knew about the German demands than in June, when only very few had been summoned, but the general public, even in Oslo, did not know anything about

the negotiations. Even the numbers of the votes were only
known in a few circles, who spread this knowledge through the
country by means of leaflets. Unfortunately, many of the
numbers given were not accurate or reliable, and this proves
how badly informed most people were. I believe that the
great majority of people still do not really know anything
about what took place, or the main trend of the negotiations.
The newspapers did not contain a single word about what was
happening, and it was first made public when Terboven made
his speech and declared that the Storting, with a two-thirds
majority, had deposed the King. Early the next morning a
well-known officer, who was very old and an ardent patriot,
came rushing into my house, nearly in despair, and asked me,
in a voice which betrayed the great anxiety in his heart: 'Is it
really true that the Storting has deposed the King with a
two-thirds majority?' He was overjoyed when I told him that
it was all nonsense. This will give some idea how
ignorant the general public was.

The negotiations lasted from Tuesday, the 10th, till
Wednesday, the 18th of September. As a member of the
committee of my own party, the Liberal Party, I was permitted
to be present all the time, and I had also the right to speak.

I will never forget the proceedings, so extraordinary and
disgusting were they. Everything was temporary, informal,
and mostly unprepared. Only the Presidential Board, the
Administrative Council—which was still functioning—and a
few politicians really knew what was going on.

Firstly, proceedings were conducted with great haste. When
the parties met on Tuesday at 11 o'clock, the Germans told us
that the proceedings must be finished by 2 o'clock. During
that terribly short space of time the chairman had to tell the
members of his party all that had happened since the 13th
June, and explain the different proposals and situations to
people who mostly knew nothing about them. The debate
was to follow, culminating in four divisions on the four
following questions:—

(1) Can we accept a settlement by agreement with the

German authorities, even if we must be content with those guarantees given by Dr. Delbrügge about the relation between the Reichskommissar and the new State Council, and even if we must vote for a Storting decision that the King and the Royal Family should withdraw?

(2) Is it possible to accept a similar settlement to that mentioned in the first question, if the decision of the Storting is that the King and the Royal Family should withdraw until the peace treaty is concluded?

(3) Are we willing to fight for a Storting decision—as mentioned in question 1—if there is a majority vote but not a qualified majority (two-thirds majority)?

(4) Are we willing to fight for a Storting decision—as mentioned in question 2—if there is a majority vote (but not a qualified majority)?

The aim of the last two questions was to secure a qualified majority in the Storting, even if it did not exist in the party meetings. In my opinion many members of the Parliament were confused and did not really understand the meaning of the questions, and they had no time to ask questions about them. At the time question 2 was not definitely formed, as I will explain later.

The Labour party unanimously asked the Germans to postpone the ballot until the evening, but they did not even receive a reply. When the members from the northern part of Norway arrived on Thursday they had to vote at once without any information, with the result that some of them, a few days afterwards, told the chairman that they had made a wrong decision in ignorance of the facts, and were not, in their opinion, committed to their votes. But they were told that their votes could not be changed.

Secondly, almost all the proceedings were oral. It was quite impossible to obtain the different questions in writing. When a member said: 'It is impossible for me to vote before I have studied the form of the proposal which will decide the future of my country for generations,' the chairman replied: 'We are in a hurry and cannot allow time for it.' The second question about the suspension of the King was not even presented in its final form. Not even the committees of the different parties were permitted to read the statement of Dr. Delbrügge about the changed conditions.

Thirdly, the parties never assembled for a joint meeting as they had asked the Germans to be allowed to do.

Fourthly, even after the Germans had broken all their June pledges, the Presidential Board felt itself committed to what they had signed on the 18th June, and they still hoped that they could obtain for the State Council a freer and more independent position than that of the Administrative Council. They were honest people, but very naïve where Nazi policy was concerned, and in September they said openly that they would never have signed the request for abdication then if they had been free. The devilish threat to send the young Norwegian men to Germany, and to execute the death sentences, and the terrible hints about a Nazi government in Norway, and about what had happened in Poland, still had a great effect upon the older politicians.

Finally, all the votes were to be preliminary under the definite understanding that the Germans, in a written communication between Terboven and the Governor Christensen, the Chairman of the future State Council, would give written guarantees in eight paragraphs.

When, in his big speech on the 25th September [1] to the Norwegian people, Reichskommissar Terboven declared that the Storting, by a qualified majority, had dethroned the King, he was uttering a shameless falsehood. The vote was temporary, there were only party meetings—the Storting did not meet in full session—and there was a majority vote against the dethronement. There were, of course, defeatists and weak-kneed persons amongst the members of the Storting, but now in September, even during the terrible attack upon London, the overwhelming majority refused to depose the King.

Again, when Terboven declared that the members of the Storting only wished to save the Government for themselves and would go in for a Nazi order, he was telling a downright lie. The great majority acted in a manner worthy of the

[1] See Appendix 4.

solemn occasion and the grave situation. I will never forget
the short discussion before the voting took place, and it was
deeply moving when one member after another stood up and
their 'No' votes rang out in the silence like the falling of an
axe. One member said: 'Now we have to prove that we meant
something when we spoke about democracy and loyalty, even
if we have to sacrifice everything.' Another member, a very
small man, said with dogged purpose and strength: 'I will not
yield a millimetre. We can never trust the Germans. My wife
will never let me into the house again if I surrender.' 'We have
to follow the star of our youth and accept all the sufferings and
sacrifices which are bound to come our way,' said another.
'We have to risk our position and our lives, be ready to go to
concentration camps or to be shot, but we will never betray
what we hold sacred, for then all our work for democracy will
have been humbug. Now we must show the people that it was
deadly earnest,' said another man. Another member said with
some emotion: 'The day I was to leave for Oslo to take part
in the debate, my three sons and two sons-in-law (who, all but
one, had taken active part in the fighting), came to me in a
body and said: "Father, you must not let Norway down, or
you can never come home again." The atmosphere was very
tense, and I replied: "No, I will not betray Norway. Not even
if they shoot me." ' Consequently the different parties of the
Storting, with a great majority, refused to break the Constitution. Fifty voted for dethronement, and eighty against, but
this majority was very much increased when the members
from the North of Norway arrived on Thursday. There is no
doubt that the majority would have been even greater if there
had been a full meeting of the Storting. Many of the members
who reluctantly voted for dethronement expressly said that
their final vote would depend upon the German guarantees.
    But then the devil appeared again with all his temptations.
    The Nazis had not succeeded in taking the Storting by a
frontal attack, so they then tried to do so by resorting to a
turning manœuvre. As I mentioned before, the second
proposal was not in its final form, and many of us, therefore,
warned our party members not to vote for it; but unfortunately

many of them did, so there was a majority for the temporary suspension of the King, until the peace was made. Seventy-five voted for question 2 and fifty-five against it. This minority was heavily increased when the members from the North voted. For question 4, which in reality was the same as question 2, about ninety voted in favour of it and about fifty against it—there was no qualified majority.

In any case these figures do not give an accurate impression of the proceedings, because nobody really understood what they were voting for. It is characteristic of the confusion that reigned that, at a dinner a few days later, three members of the Parliament who were present, all of whom had voted against the question, presented three entirely different views of the situation. The intention of the voters was merely to state the fact that the King and the Government, living outside Norway, could not exercise their constitutional functions in Norway, and they made this fact quite clear. Many had heard that the Germans would not accept question 2, and therefore they did not think there was any risk in voting for it temporarily. They were, therefore, horrified the next day when they got the final form, which declared that the King had forfeited his crown. They openly protested, with great vehemence, that they were not committed at all by their votes, but the Germans said that they could not withdraw from a vote which was only intended to be a preliminary. Then the Norwegian negotiators under pressure tried to persuade the party members, secretly and individually, to stand by their votes, and a few of them, through loyalty to their party leaders, withdrew their protests. It is therefore very difficult to state what was the actual final number of votes.

The Germans did not break off the negotiations, in spite of the fact that their offensive had not been successful. They tried shuffling the cards as much as possible, to confuse the issue even more. Their aim was to confuse everything, and to make everything as hazy as possible, so that the Norwegians could be foiled into accepting terms which the Germans could later interpret as meaning that the Norwegians had deposed the King. The Presidential Board tried to find a form of compromise by which the King would resign until the end of the war, when he would automatically take up his functions again, but the Germans refused to allow this, and during the following days a tug-of-war took place between the Norwegians and the Germans. The latter had really unveiled their intentions when they proposed that the State Council, and not the Presidential Board, should, in the case of seats becoming vacant, appoint the new members. If this motion had been adopted, the Storting would have committed suicide, and the Germans could have filled the State Council with Quislings, dismissed the chairman, Mr. Christensen, and the real Norwegians, and by these cunning means have legalized the Quisling regime. It was just in this way that Hitler had destroyed German parliamentary life, when he persuaded the different parties to give him a blank cheque and afterwards dissolved them. This was, therefore, a major question, and neither of the two sides would yield.

On Saturday, the 14th September, Terboven returned, together with Quisling, from Berlin. The Fuehrer would not concede anything. He had now rejected Mr. Ringnes, a Norwegian Germanophil, and his personal guest at his fiftieth birthday celebrations, as a candidate for the Ministry of Foreign Affairs, because he was strongly against Quisling and had called him a liar, and replaced him by Captain Irgens, who in his heart was a Nazi and later became one of the Kommissars in the Government. This fact was very illuminating. The Quislings now had at least four members in the future State Council, and they would certainly obtain a few more. Gradually, therefore, they would be able to get rid of the honest members and supplant them with their own partisans. It is very illuminating of the Quisling mentality that Captain Irgens had given his word of honour to Mr. Christensen that he did not belong to Nasjonal Samling. Therefore, the Presidential Board now asked the prospective Minister of Police, Jonas Lie, to appear before them because many people suspected him of being a real Nazi. They asked him about his relation to Quisling and Nasjonal Samling. Lie answered: 'I never belonged to his party, I don't do so now, and I will never join it, because I do not agree with their ideology.' This answer was given to all the different parties, and only a few days later Jonas Lie appeared in the new Quisling government, and even took part as a leader of the so-called Regiment Nordland, in the war against Greece, and was decorated with the Iron Cross. He then became known as Judas with the Iron Cross from the war of liberation of the Greeks!

I know the Nazi methods well, but during these negotiations I was simply horrified to find how low German political culture had sunk. The most scandalous moment was when the Germans said on Monday, 16th September,: 'Well, about the King, the State Council and so on, you may vote on the Norwegian text of the proposal, but it is the German text which will be valid.' Now the German draft was substantially different from the Norwegian, and it was just this difference which was in dispute. I shall never forget how wholeheartedly many of the elected representatives of the Norwegian people refused to betray the democratic ideals of their homeland. In my party group everybody voted against it, and when the result was made known there was a great shout of delight, and we all shook hands enthusiastically, and congratulated one another. Now we felt sure that the great rupture in the negotiations, for which we longed, would come about. But in the afternoon the whole situation had changed, and it became apparent that the votes of the other parties had been made on a different basis.

Still many representatives, hoping against hope that they could obtain a real Norwegian administration, tried to compromise, and many of us really feared a disastrous result. Very few of the people knew anything about the negotiations, which were confidential, but some prominent people tried to influence the political leaders. For instance, General Ruge, our Commander-in-Chief, who was still a prisoner in a villa near Oslo, because he refused to give the Germans his word of honour, secretly sent the different parties the following message: 'The battle which is now going on in the air over Britain is the battle of the Marne. If the Germans have not taken London by the end of September, they will definitely lose the war. Therefore, don't give way. Stand firm.'

Tuesday, the 17th September, was the turning point in the negotiations. In the letter to Terboven from Mr. Christensen, as the prospective chairman of the State Council, which was read aloud to the members of the different political parties on Monday, Christensen demanded guarantees that the Council of State would have a much freer position than the Administrative Council, and that the whole arrangement would only be a temporary one. The State Council should govern according to the law of the country, the Reichskommissar should not interfere directly in the civil administration of Norway, the Norwegian principle of law should be maintained in the press, broadcasting, theatres, cinemas, and by all publishers; the political parties should be placed on an equal footing with each other; and the financial basis of Norway should not be destroyed. Finally Christensen also asked an amnesty for people who were in prison or under sentence. When the reply about the guarantees was submitted to Mr. Christensen and the Presidential Board, the German letter was found to be so vague in form and so unsatisfactory in character, that the Presidential Board plainly told the Germans that, in its present form, it could not form a basis for the decision of the Storting. The Germans always gave with one hand and took away with the other. All the most important paragraphs were made dependent on conditions which made everything illusory, 'provided that these rules are not contrary to the interest of the German Reich' or 'we presume they are in accordance with the interpretation of the Reichskommissar'. The same day, they demanded that the prospective Minister of Justice, Mr. Harbech, who was a reliable and patriotic Norwegian, should be replaced by a member of the Quisling party.

Now, at last, the members of the Presidential Board and Government, and Christensen suddenly understood what had really happened. Hitherto, they had been completely blind, but this last German trick opened their eyes, and they were amazed to see that they were standing on the brink of a precipice. They firmly resisted this new demand, the intention of which was to nazify the State Council. The following day, Terboven broke off the negotiations, but in reality the rupture was due to the Storting itself, a fact which was joyously hailed throughout the country. Even if many members had gone too far in concessions, the Storting, as an institution, had not surrendered and profaned its glorious traditions, and nearly all the members went home feeling very relieved that the negotiations had been broken off, even if they also understood that now a very dark period would follow.

The Nazis had lost the battle, they had failed in their attempt to threaten the Norwegians to violate their Constitution. Now they dropped the mask, and Terboven in his speech bluntly told the people that he had obtained all the things which, in reality, the Storting had rejected. He told another terrible lie when he said that the members of the Parliament had been willing to sacrifice everything, and to condemn the Government, in order to keep their own seats. This question was never even raised during the negotiations with the different political parties. Terboven also said that he broke off the negotiations when the members of Parliament tried, by legal tricks, to gain a decisive influence over the State Council. He was referring to the insistence of Parliament that the Presidential Board should supplement the State Council.

Another version of the cause of the rupture in the negotiations was given by the German High Command in Norway in a letter of 28th September, 1940, found in Lofoten. In this letter the High Command said that the development in the political situation since April, 1940, had shown that, with the exception of the Nasjonal Samling party, 'all other organizations and parties, and particularly the representatives of big business and industrials remain, now as before, pro-English, and consequently anti-German, and that the Norwegian people and their former leaders are at present in no position to adapt themselves to the political situation, and to fulfil the demands of the New Era. In spite of repeatedly proffered opportunities of taking over the control of domestic politics in their own country, the Norwegians have continued only to make a pretence of falling in with these offers. At the critical moment, however, they have always refused to shoulder the responsibility, and are consequently pursuing a deliberate policy of "hold-back" and "wait-and-see" in order to gain time.

'In consideration of this development and obstruction and of the necessity, due to the approach of winter, of solving without delay numerous tasks of vital importance for the country, Reichskommissar Terboven decided to break off negotiations.'

Even then it was a week before anything happened. The Quislings had great difficulties in getting qualified members for the new Administration. They represent a very small and unimportant minority of our people. They have no brains at all, and most of them are either crazy persons with an inferiority complex, people who have never succeeded in life, or wrecks from the former great economic crises. In Oslo these days were full of suspense and had a very sombre and macabre character, especially after Monday, 23rd September, when Terboven, without consulting the Administrative Council, suddenly dismissed the head of Police in Oslo, Mr. Welhaven, and replaced him by a Quisling. Although the people did not know anything, they had a feeling that something dreadful, something which would decide their own personal fate, as well as that of their country, was about to happen. In every home in every part of Norway, for the first time, people were anxiously listening in to hear what Terboven would tell them in his broadcast. They had been informed in the newspapers that Terboven would speak. I was a guest in Oslo at the monthly Cod Dinner of the Sailors' Association, on the 25th September, and I shall never forget the scene when all those Captains and sea-dogs were standing round the radio listening to the speech of the Reichskommissar Terboven in German—followed by a translation in Norwegian. They listened first with sorrow to his declaration about the King, and then with rising anger. I can still see those hundreds of men, hard-looking, swarthy, stubborn, standing with their fists clenched and with a look of resolute determination on their faces; they presented, as always, a true picture of the Norwegian people.

In his insulting and mendacious speech [1] Reichskommissar Terboven proclaimed that henceforth Norway was to be administered as a German Protectorate and declared that the King and the Royal Family were dethroned, the legal Government dismissed, the Storting was finished with, and the Administrative Council was terminated. All Norwegian parties were to be dissolved immediately and only the Quisling party, Nasjonal Samling, which had never succeeded in obtaining more than 2 per cent of Norwegian public votes, and had never won a single representative elected to the Storting, would be permitted to exist ; but the Norwegian system of administration was to be preserved, declared the German High Command, in the previously quoted letter. At the same time Terboven appointed 13 members of a 'cabinet', composed exclusively of Quisling's supporters and sympathizers. Only a few of them had any experience in political life or were qualified as administrative leaders. The inaugural declaration with which Terboven provided his new Council (not the State Council) stated openly that Norway was to be a unit in the German Lebensraum, that the foreign policy of the country and even all questions of foreign *trade* were to be decided in Berlin. Quisling himself was not a member of the Government of Kommissars, but he adopted the name *Fuehrer*. He was head of the Nasjonal Samling and had influence behind the scenes only as the future Prime Minister or Gauleiter, if and when the Nazis had subdued the Norwegian people. [2]

[1] See Appendix 4.

[2] I lived in the same house as Quisling—but, fortunately, we had different entrances—and I had the opportunity of closely following his activities from the 9th April until the 25th September. He had only two members of his own party acting as guards during the night, and his chauffeur never left him—always accompanying him right up the staircase to his flat, and coming right to his flat to fetch him every time he went out. But from the 25th September it was quite different. During the day two Norwegian policemen stood guard outside the main entrance, and two more at the back entrance, and during the night they were joined by members of his own party, and people who lived in the house and used this entrance had to have identity cards which had to be shown to the guards before they were allowed to pass through.

The thirteen heads of the various government departments were called 'constituted kommissars (*kommissarische Staatsräte*) —a title which the public at once paraphrased as 'prostituted kommissars', since that designation, in the opinion of the man-in-the-street, more accurately covered their duties. In accordance with the decree of Reichskommissar Terboven, each 'constituted kommissar' was *officially empowered*—within his department and within the limits of his activities as drawn up by the representatives of the occupying nation—to make all decisions alone, to appoint or dismiss officials, to change, supplement, or even revoke laws previously in force. And now the weeding out of Norwegian democrats, in public offices and in cultural institutions at once began. Immediately three Governors of Provinces were replaced by Quislings, and the chairman of the Trades Union Congress, Mr. Volan, who, in the negotiations with the Germans, had conceded nearly everything in order to appease them, was dismissed, and more willing Trades Union leaders who in former days had been expelled from the Labour Party, or people who were willing to co-operate in the 'new order' were brought in.

The so-called Norwegian Government was not a government. They did not meet as a corporative body. Terboven had complete authority over them and they were responsible only to him.[1] The Germans had at last taken over the complete power with the assistance of a few Norwegian traitors and opportunists, who represented only a very insignificant part of the people. The Nazis and the Quislings had completely broken down the Eidsvold Constitution and only the Supreme Court still existed, because the Nazis declared that they would respect the Norwegian law. The Norwegian people were still rallying to the King and the legal Government, and did not pay any attention to the decree stating that activities in support of the Royal House, the Government and the former political parties were strictly forbidden. They loathed the name of Quisling. His 'new order' was simply a forced order, created and supported only

[1] Later on the Nazis' iron grip became firmer and firmer. The Commissars were not able to do anything unless the Nazis sanctioned it.

E

by the German military power and the Gestapo. There had
been no revolution. If left to themselves, the Quislings would
not have survived a day, not even for five minutes. Now a
terrible period of suffering, oppression, and persecution
began.

CHAPTER 6

Norway under the Nazi Kommissars

1. The Assault on Norway's Cultural Life

FROM the very first day of its existence, the Nazi Kommissariat was in a state of open warfare against practically the entire Norwegian population. This state of affairs began with the threat of 'drastic measures' against all who refused to submit to the new order, and with the turning loose in the streets of Nazi youths, who were permitted to engage in provocative acts against everyone.

As early as the 24th September, Quisling's young Storm-troopers, or Hirdmen, suddenly attacked the students in their assembly room at the university. They were badly beaten and had to call for help not only from the Norwegian police, but also from the German soldiers. Later on in many cities they very often attacked innocent people in the streets. They swooped on schools to punish teachers or young pupils who demonstrated against them. And in the last days of April they kidnapped the Head Surgeon of a big mental hospital outside Oslo, because he refused to appoint a member of the Nazi party as hospital superintendent, and arrested him without any order. The trouble started when the Nazi-appointed surgeon-general of Norway announced that all appointments of municipal and district doctors would be determined by their political views. The other sixteen head doctors of all the hospitals in Oslo protested against this terrible breach of the law, and threatened to resign if the head surgeon of the mental hospital was not set free immediately. 'If this categorical demand is not met,' they declared, 'and if we are not given complete freedom and protection under the law to care for the sick, then we shall feel obliged to resign from our positions.'[1]

[1] On the 25th of June the head doctors won a decisive victory. The Head Surgeon of the mental hospital was reinstated; the German authorities promised to remove the hospital superintendent and forbade the Hird in the future to interfere with the hospitals.

It is estimated that there are a thousand of these Norwegian Nazis in Norway. While the membership formerly consisted of many High School pupils and office workers, most new recruits have been found amongst the anti-social and criminal elements of the population, potential gangsters who are now paid wages for performing deeds for which neither the Norwegian police nor the courts can hold them accountable.

The principles of Norway's democratic Constitution of 1814 were thus trampled under foot. Officially it was stated that the independence of the courts of law would be respected, but at the same time the Kommissars established a so-called Public Court of Justice which was to decide political cases, and as President of the court they appointed a party member, a very unimportant lawyer, who had already shown that he lacked the most elementary knowledge of law. Judges were dismissed and new ones, of a very inferior type, appointed. Even the Attorney-General is now reported to have been arrested because he refused to greet one of the new, illegally appointed judges. The Constituted Minister of Justice even went so far as to defend the principle of retaliation when the Hirdmen attacked Norwegian youths.

In the beginning the Kommissars did not dare to remove many people from the Civil Service, which was then in operation and still is. The policy of the Civil Service at first was to wait and see, and in this way it tried to prevent the worst excesses of the Quislings. One reason why the Kommissars did not interfere with them immediately was that they had very few people whom they could put into the Civil Service. By and by, however, the Kommissars tried to get rid of the anti-Nazi officials by lowering the retiring age and by other tricks. They also dismissed some people outright, but the number of people dismissed was very small compared with the size of the organization. Many of the people who in this way were dismissed or forced to retire were supported by private funds—mainly by private individuals—so that this emergency was met. It was of the utmost importance that as few people as possible should be forced, by reason of economic pressure, to join the Quislings.

The Kommissars also tried to dissolve the local organs of self-government and to introduce the Fuehrer principle, with the result that chaos ensued in most of the municipal administrations. Only the Mayor, who was now appointed and not elected, was entitled to make decisions, and the members of the local councils were permitted only to express their opinions. A number of new Mayors were now appointed—as the Quislings had few competent candidates, they had reluctantly to ask the old mayors to continue in office—but many refused to accept office and it proved very difficult for the Quislings to set up a new machine, because all branches lacked experienced people. In March, the Public Court of Justice condemned sixteen members of the Labour Party in the Oslo Town Council to fifteen or eighteen month's imprisonment, because they had protested against the violation of the law of local government.

The Kommissars interfered with the schools and ordered the teachers to co-operate in a positive manner in spreading Nazi propaganda, and even to protect the young asses who were beaten by their comrades because of their pro-Nazi sympathies. Several teachers who refused to do this were removed from their posts or arrested. The Kommissars then began to warn all the principals of schools against using certain textbooks in English which, they said, might have very undesirable effects on the pupils. They also made the heads of the schools responsible for seeing that so-called anti-German propaganda did not take place.

The German Gestapo Chief informed the Rector of the University that the attitude of the University should not only be correct, but also friendly towards Germany and German politics. The Quisling administration dismissed Professors and appointed new ones, but the students stood firm and would not listen to them. And when the only Nazi Professor of Medicine tried to remove his enemy, one of the foremost Professors in Medicine, all the professors in all the faculties threatened to resign. He was recently given six months' leave because no students attended his lectures. Lectures given by German professors or supporters of the Nasjonal Samling are systematically boycotted by the students.

The Nazis immediately dissolved the old Students' Association which from 1813 had always played a leading part in affairs on the national front. The Gestapo arrested the young President and his wife, and the famous Dr. Scharffenberg, the specialist in mental diseases, who had written many articles against the Nazis and had declared Hitler himself insane. He was an idealist who always tried to find the truth, without any regard to his former opinions. As one of the leaders of the Republicans in 1905, he made a great speech to the Students' Association about what had happened in the year when the King was elected, and paid a fervent tribute to the loyalty and courage of the King who was now the foremost champion of liberty and national freedom. I was present at that meeting and I will never forget how nearly a thousand young students rose, time and again to cheer the King with wild enthusiasm and to protest against the German demand for his deposition.

The Church too had to suffer. The Quislings ordered the use of a new Common Prayerbook from which the prayer of intercession for the King and his house, and for the King's Cabinet, had been eliminated. The police department published an order abolishing the professional oath of secrecy taken by Ministers, lawyers, physicians, and surgeons, and employees in the telegraph and telephone offices, and imposing a penalty of imprisonment for refusing to supply the police with information.

One of the first acts of the Quislings was to 'gleichschalten' the wireless and the press. The newspapers were ordered to print only Nazi propaganda and to refrain from giving any news or views favourable to the Allied cause. They eventually went so far as to confiscate the offices and printing works of the big newspapers, and to stop newspapers which they disliked or to change their names and run them themselves. By December, 1940, at least thirty-five newspapers had ceased publication. Numbers of Norwegian journalists were arrested without the benefit of trial before any court. Some of them

were even sent to concentration camps in Germany. The
Germans then began to search the printing works, to try to
discover illegal literature and leaflets, and they even appeared
suddenly in the trams and demanded that people should show
them what they were carrying in their cases. They have not
only forbidden us to read Einstein, but even our most famous
authoress, Sigrid Undset. During 1940 they confiscated about
three hundred books written by foreign authors, and have
forbidden the sale of the book about the visit of the Crown
Prince and Princess to America. In the propaganda department they are now preparing a list of Norwegian literature
which is to be banned and confiscated.

They tried to gain entrance into many important trade
organizations, in order to use them as instruments of
nazification.

In collaboration with the Germans, the so-called new and
loyal leadership was set up over the Trades Union Congress.
The Union members were strongly opposed to any concessions being made, and several officials refused to collaborate
with the new leaders and were, therefore, compelled to withdraw. Fearing a strike in the important military works, the
Germans refused to support the demand made by Quisling
that the Labour Unions should be forced, collectively, to join
the National Union. Workmen and labourers in all trades and
industries have made it clear, at the risk of their lives, that they
intend to resist any attempts at nazification to their utmost.
One local Union expressed this resolution forcibly by rejecting,
in the proportion of 5,000 to sixteen, the proposed vote of
loyalty to the newly appointed Nazi Labour official in their
National organization. The Quislings have tried to bribe some
sections of the industrial workers with higher wages, but the
bribe has had very little effect, since the workers find that
although they have more paper money in their pockets, there
is nothing to buy with it. At the same time the closing down
of many factories and short-time working in others, owing to
the shortage of coal and other raw materials and fuels, has
more than counterbalanced the effect of the nominal wage
increases. As a result, the opposition of the workers is growing

steadily from month to month. In general it takes the form of 'going slow' in the factories.

The Association of Fishermen have declared themselves willing to co-operate in production, but they have refused categorically to admit representatives of the Nasjonal Samling to their Board of Directors. The farmers also adopted the same attitude and therefore the President of the Farmers' Association, Mr. Mellbye, a former Minister of Agriculture, who was one of Hitler's honorary birthday guests, has been dismissed from his position as President, after lifelong service in this association for the benefit of the Norwegian farmers, and has been placed in confinement in his house in the country. The Nazis also dismissed the General Secretary and other important members of the Central Committee, and replaced them with ardent supporters of the Nazis.

Following the tradition of their forefathers, the former leaders refused to bow humbly to foreign oppressors acting in open violation of Norwegian and International law.

The attempt to bribe the farmers and the fishermen with higher prices has also had little effect generally. The Nazi party organ, *Free People*, devoted a recent editorial to the stubborn refusal of the Norwegian farmers to accept the new situation, and proposed, as a solution, that they should be 'sent to concentration camps along with the Jews'.

The Association of Norwegian Shipowners, which occupies a unique position, was declared dissolved, its leaders were imprisoned, its offices taken over, and its large funds seized. The Nazis have also tried to force the shipowners, personally, to recall their ships, but without any result. However, even if the shipowners had obeyed them, the captains of the ships would never have listened to the orders coming from Oslo. The explanation of this action against the Shipowners' Association is, of course, that the Germans are furious and worried about the very great services which the Norwegian Merchant Navy of about 4 million tons and 25,000 sailors is performing daily for the Allied cause. On the other hand, it has been a very great encouragement to the sailors that the

(*Above*) A scene in Oslo's most famous street. Note the German soldiers in the foreground.

OSLO UNDER THE NAZIS

(*Below*) A queue in front of a meat shop.

NORWAY'S MEAT SHORTAGE

This butcher's shop has no meat to sell and is closed

German soldiers on sentry in front of the *Storting* (the
Norwegian Parliament).

shipowners at home have taken such a firm stand, worthy of a seafaring nation.

The Nazis have also tried to gain control of the strong organization of 300,000 active athletes, by appointing Sports Leaders. On the 22nd November, 1940, it was announced that the Quislings would take over the organization of Norwegian sport, and that all independent associations would be dissolved. This produced a nation-wide rebellion against the enforced Nazi reorganization of the formerly democratic associations of skiers and of other sports groups. The leaders of Norwegian sport sent a strong protest to the Kommissar, in which they declared that they had no intention of abandoning their 'legal, moral, and financial responsibilities'. Letters and telegrams in support of this protest poured in from all over the country. When the duly elected leaders were replaced by minor puppets of the Quisling regime—practically all the well-known sportsmen refused the 'honour' of being nominated leaders—thousands upon thousands of young Norwegians showed their displeasure and contempt by refusing to participate in any of the athletic competitions which were organized by them. Most significant of all, the ski-ing contests at Holmenkollen, outside Oslo, were a complete fiasco. Major Helseth, a very popular and highly respected sports leader and former President of the Norwegian Sports Association, was then arrested, but this only further consolidated the opposition of these young men and women, representing some of the most able and active elements in Norwegian society.

The Germans also tried to force the medical organizations into the Nasjonal Samling, but they did not succeed and met with stubborn resistance.

Attempts were also made to control the theatres more strictly; the police issued a new order in which actors were not only strictly forbidden to add anything that was not in their original scripts, which might be offensive to the German army and the Nasjonal Samling, but also strictly forbidden to offend them in any way by gestures, insinuating pauses, inflexions of the voice, or anything of this kind. After the 25th September, even the Royal box at the National Theatre in Oslo was no longer respected. The theatre was now forced to sell it as an ordinary box. However, the first time that anyone was bold enough to appear in it there was a terrible uproar. The audience expressed their feelings by booing and hissing to such a degree that the party in the box had to leave the theatre before the performance could begin. A few days later, having taken Gestapo and police precautions, six Germans bought seats in the Royal box; but this was even worse, for the public just left the theatre. After that, for a long time, a little boy went every morning and bought the box, so that no one should sit in it.

The strict decrees against the actors did not frighten them, however, and they continued to try to give expression, as far as possible, to the feelings of the nation. For instance, in the Spring of 1941, in a revue at the Chat Noir, one of the acts consisted of an actor, dressed in the full uniform of an Admiral—he was very tall and not unlike King Haakon— simply walking slowly across the stage, without saying a word. The audience understood his meaning immediately, and it was impossible to stop their cheering and shouting. Then the actor put his head round the curtain and said: 'Do you want me to come back again?' The answering 'Yes' from the audience nearly lifted the roof off the theatre.

The next day the actor and his manager were summoned to the Nazi controller of the theatre and rebuked. In the evening this act was cut out of the show—the actor was not permitted 'to come back again.'

Many such demonstrations took place in the different theatres. The real meaning of seemingly the most innocent remark was caught by the audience, who demonstrated their appreciation and approval. The Kommissar of Police, on 5th May, therefore repeated the order to the Chiefs of Police all over the country, to censor all public theatrical productions and all artistic recitations. No plays, not even the classic Norwegian dramas, could be performed if they could in any way be interpreted as relating to the present situation or to the war. Jewish or modern British plays were absolutely banned.

American plays could only be performed in the rare cases when they were of a nature which, in Nazi terminology, could be described as 'positive' from the ethical and moral point of view.

The Germans even tried to force actors to take part in propaganda sketches and radio plays for the Nazi party. The Norwegian people had refused to listen to Norwegian radio broadcasts from Norwegian stations, and now the actors were to be used as bait for Nazi propaganda. If the actors did not obey, they were forbidden to follow their profession either in Norway or to go abroad, but all the actors, except one or two, combined to form a common front and declared that they would use their free time as they liked. On 21st May six of the best-known actors and actresses, who had refused to broadcast, were summoned—one by one—to the Gestapo Headquarters for an inquiry. The Gestapo told them that if they still refused to broadcast they would not be permitted to continue their artistic careers, as their refusal would be regarded as a demonstration of a hostile attitude towards the 'new order'. The actors were also informed that, as part of their punishment, they would be forbidden to receive economic support, in any form, from the Actors' Association, or from anybody else. All the actors, however, stood firmly by their decision, and stuck to their principle that actors had a right to dispose of their free time as they wished. It is reported that the Germans were very perplexed by the actors' stubbornness, but, nevertheless, they carried out their threat. On 23rd May the Actors' Association had a meeting at which the six disqualified members appeared. These six members declared that although they would appreciate all evidence of solidarity from the other members of the Association, they felt they must emphasize that it was not possible to calculate what consequences would have to be borne by every single member if this evidence were forthcoming, and they therefore asked their colleagues not to take any decision which was influenced by their personal regard for them. The gathering decided with 118 votes to sixteen to go on strike and to refuse to act as a protest. There was absolute unanimity in their condemnation of the action taken against these six members by the Gestapo, as the minority of sixteen did not vote from political motives but simply from practical ones. On 25th May seven actors were arrested, as chosen representatives of the various theatres in Oslo.

As a consequence of these arrests the theatres in Oslo, Bergen and Trondheim had closed down by the end of May. This strike was followed by further arrests. Moreover the funds belonging to the association were seized and steps were taken to 'freeze' the actors' private accounts.

Consequently the Quislings decided to nazify the theatres, and all theatres are now being placed under the control of the Department of 'Culture and Enlightenment'. A licensing system has been introduced both for actors and theatres. Licensed actors will be required to sign a new contract pledging them to collaborate with all state cultural institutions. Actors who refuse to take part in nazi-controlled films and broadcasts—as did these six actors whose disqualification was the cause of the strike—will henceforth, under the decree, be deprived of their livelihood.

Every theatre is to have a 'Leader' responsible to the Quisling Kommissar for Education. His task will be to see that Norwegian theatres work in conformity with the 'New Order'.

But nothing apparently, could break the resistance of the Norwegian actors. The Nazis then went a step further; on the 26th June they arrested four very prominent citizens of Oslo because, as directors of the National Theatre, they refused to ask the quisling 'Ministry for Culture and Enlightenment' for a licence. The arrested directors were: Professor Francis Bull, chairman of the board of directors and Professor of Nordic Literature at the Oslo University; Hr. Harald Grieg, managing director of the well-known publishing house of Gyldendal and chairman of the Norwegian Publishers' Association; Hr. Jens P. Heyerdahl, a leading barrister of the Supreme Court and chairman of one of the leading Norwegian banks; and Hr. Sejersted Bödtker, a leading banker and art collector.

At the same time the Nazis threatened that if these arrests were announced through the B.B.C.'s Norwegian broadcast these people would be interned in a concentration camp. The German authorities also threatened that all the Norwegian theatres would be taken over by the German military authorities, and would be used as barracks for German soldiers, or as store-houses. At the beginning of July, however, the strike was called off, and the actors returned to their theatres. They did it mainly to help their arrested colleagues. They were informed that the arrested actors and actresses would shortly be set free; no conditions were definitely stated or agreed upon, but the Germans promised that from now on the actors would not be forced to take part in any activity of a political or propaganda nature. The arrested directors were also set free, but after only a few days arrested again.

There were also demonstrations in the cinemas. For instance, in Trondheim the film depicting the bombing and destruction of Rotterdam was shown, and the public simply would not have it. They booed and whistled, stamped and shouted until the lights were turned up. A German Colonel, in full uniform, rose and tried to reason with the turbulent house, but they would not let him have his say. The Colonel lost his temper and ordered everyone to go home. Then the cinema boycott began. In many towns people refused to attend the cinemas for weeks on end, and the popular indignation against the Stormtroopers' practice of entering theatres without paying, increased. Leaflets stating that no true and loyal Norwegian should go to the cinema were distributed. The strike was very effective, and the cinemas in Oslo in the Spring of 1941 only took 30 per cent of their usual box office receipts. When the Norwegians did go to the movies, their behaviour during 'enlightenment films' was so deplorable that the Quislings issued strict orders forbidding all demonstrations.

The act of 'demonstrating' was defined as including the following points of behaviour:—

(1) Laughter.

(2) 'Meaningless applause' (i.e. clapping at the wrong places in the film).

(3) Stamping with the feet.

(4) Whistling.

(5) Coughing.

(6) 'Harking' (the expressive Norwegian word for clearing one's throat).

The German attempt to recruit people for a 'Nordland Regiment', which was to fight side by side with the Germans, was a complete failure. It was impossible to form even a battalion. In order to get together a few hundred soldiers they had to order local Stormtroops to supply men from their own forces, and to raise the age-limit.

All in all the attitude of Norwegians of all trades and professions can be summed up in the motto published by a brave Stavanger editor who, together with his staff, was arrested after he had published it: 'No Norwegian is for sale!'

And now persecution of the Jews has begun. Early every morning in the autumn, a party of students went to the Jewish shops—there were not many of them—and painted out the insulting slogans on their windows.

At the same time Nazi terrorism has been increasing. Hundreds of people have been arrested and put into prison or sent to concentration camps without any trial whatsoever, and the Gestapo, which at the turn of the year 1940–41 employed between nine to ten thousand of its own people in Norway, creeps like a dark shadow everywhere, introducing their third-degree methods. You can never feel safe: either late in the afternoon or early in the morning the Gestapo suddenly appear to make arrests, generally on suspicion or on information provided by spies. Often mistakes are made and people sit in prison for months before these are discovered. Waiters, for example, are bribed to act as informers, to tell the Gestapo who is speaking with whom at the different tables and to listen to conversations. Long distance telephone calls are always tapped, also all telephone calls of any person whom the Gestapo wishes to control. Arrests are now so frequently issued, that there is no disgrace attached to them. They are now taken so much as a matter of course, that it is said that Norwegians keep their suitcases packed, ready to go.

In some cases it has been reported that conditions of life in prison have been fairly comfortable, especially at the beginning; a great deal depended upon the prison wardens, but later on the control of the prisons was taken over by more brutal young men from the Gestapo. These younger members of the Gestapo instituted a form of exercise in the corridors of the various prisons—exercises which were very exhausting for older people. Maltreatment in the prisons is not usual, according to reliable reports. In two concentration camps, one at Oslo and the other at Bergen, the treatment has been more brutal. On several occasions prisoners have been forced to stand barefoot in the snow, and, to force them to confess, shots were then fired as near to their legs as it was possible to fire without actually hitting them. Prisoners suspected of serious offences, have been subjected to extremely severe mental pressure. For example, they are forbidden to receive visitors, to send or receive letters, or even to enjoy the relaxation of smoking. In some cases reading the Bible is also forbidden. Sometimes prisoners have been questioned for nine or ten hours, or more, and awakened every half hour during the night. In the prisons of Oslo, a few cases of attempted suicide have been reported, a few prisoners have gone mad, and many—including the famous author Ronald Fangen,[1] who was taken to a mental hospital—have had nervous breakdowns. These cases may have been due to confinement in completely darkened cells. Maltreatment of prisoners has also taken place whilst they were being questioned by the Gestapo. Indescribable procedures have been reported, which resulted in the victims being sent to hospital with cracked ribs, broken jaws or noses, burst ear-drums, or in a state of complete nervous breakdown. On being released some of them are forced to sign a declaration stating that they will not disclose what has

---

[1] He was released on 27th June, after the attack upon Russia, because the Nazis then tried to persuade the Norwegians that their real aim was the destruction of Bolshevism.

happened to them during their imprisonment. Political offenders who are sentenced to more than three months' imprisonment are transported to German prisons to serve their term there. Others remain in Norwegian prisons, or concentration camps, where the treatment up to now has supposedly been much better than in Germany. The following story illustrates the Nazi terror tactics: 'After a bombing raid by the R.A.F. on the aluminium plants at Hoyanger, on the Sogne Fjord, four unexploded bombs were discovered by the Germans. Nazi authorities informed the local population that these bombs were extremely dangerous and that they would have to be removed. No German life would, however, be placed in jeopardy, the Nazi commandant said. He then sent word to the prison where the ten Norwegian patriots who had been sentenced to death some time ago were kept, ordering a number of them to be brought to the spot. Pointing to the unexploded bombs the commandant told the prisoners to remove and destroy them. 'You are already under sentence of death,' he said, 'and you have not much to lose.'

'These loyal Norwegians, rank amateurs in the field of explosives, accepted the sadistic challenge without hesitation, and successfully removed the bombs; whereupon they were brought back to prison. Two of the men who thus put the Nazis to shame were the well-known editors in Stavanger, Christian S. Oftedal and Fritjof Lund, who, together with eight others, were sentenced to death on 24th February, 1941, allegedly because they had been instrumental in handing over military secrets to the British.'

All organs of the Norwegian police are forbidden to interfere for or against members of the Nasjonal Samling or the Body-guard organization. If they take any stand or action against Quisling demonstrators it will lead to the most severe punishment. Many of these policemen tried to resign when they received these orders and had to give the Nazi salute when on duty. In Oslo a hundred officers refused to go on duty until they were threatened with transportation to concentration camps in Germany, while in Christiansand fifty-nine out of sixty-two men resigned rather than obey Nazi rulings. In other cities the police force have continued to function, even under the difficult conditions imposed by the occupation forces, because they say it is better to have Norwegians than Nazis as policemen.

The Germans have now condemned three more people to death in Bergen, for espionage. Later, in February, also in Bergen, ten more people were condemned for the same reason. They were all so dignified and courageous that the German officers said afterwards that they would have been proud if they had been Germans. But they have only executed those Norwegians who have killed German soldiers.

In any case, these sentences did not lessen the resistance of the rest of the population. In March, therefore, Terboven made a great effort to put an end, once and for all, to this national, underground work and these national demonstrations, by increasing the punishment for such offences by imposing the death sentence, hard labour, or imprisonment on the slightest pretext. Without a formal declaration of martial law this proclamation, in fact, imposes martial law on Norway in a ruthless form, which violates all the principles of international law applying to the activities of an occupying power. German law, from now on, was to be applied to all offences either against the German forces or against an authority established by order of the Fuehrer and Reich Chancellor. The offences include such things as 'interference with the smooth working of any undertaking of importance to the German defence of Norway and to the Norwegian people's supplies . . . weakening the fighting spirit of the German soldiers in any way . . . attempting to leave Norway in order to enter an anti-German military force or organization . . . and, doing any kind of service to a citizen of Great Britain or the British Empire'. This, however, has not had the desired effect, or in fact shown any results at all.

2. The Assault on Norway's Standard of Living

The fact that the confiscation of food and stores of all kinds continues and that the Germans are revealing more and more plainly their plans to make Norway a German colony, has not

F

contributed to the amelioration of relations between the Norwegians and the occupying power.

From the first day of the invasion, Norway has been systematically robbed by the Germans. They buy up all sorts of products without rationing themselves. They steadily reduce the Norwegian standard of living, allowing the Norwegians just enough to keep alive. They have always paid for what they have taken, but the payment has been made in Norwegian paper money printed on their instructions and worth only the goods one can obtain for it.

And the goods are now becoming scarcer and scarcer, in spite of the huge stocks of all the most important commodities which were stored in the country when the Germans arrived, especially petrol, oil, coal, grain and coffee.

There is now practically no petrol left in Norway for her own consumption. The automobile traffic has practically ceased to exist. Only Quislings can obtain supplies of petrol for their private cars. In Oslo, for instance, there are now gasolene-run taxis, and not many of these. Crude oil—mainly used by the fishing fleet—has, however, been supplied by the Germans, not out of any love for the Norwegian fishermen but because fish was and is an essential commodity for the Germans themselves. All the stocks of dried fish were at once taken over by the Germans. Most of the herring catch is used by the Germans for the production of oils for use both as edible fats and in the manufacture of ammunition. The fish oil plants have, therefore, been taken over by the Germans to make up for their shortage of whale oil. Sixty per cent of all fresh fish goes to Germany, but what is left has been enough to fill the growing emptiness in the larder of the Norwegian housewife, though it is very expensive. Fish and fish products seem, so far, to have saved the greater part of the Norwegian population from actual want, but during recent weeks in Oslo there have been queues even in front of the fishmongers. The high price of equipment prevented many fishermen from carrying on their work, and many preferred to work on the land instead of fishing.

Steamship traffic around the coast has been very limited

owing to lack of coal, and the same applies to the railways. Very seldom now do the trains run on time; this is due to bad coal or to the fact that the rolling stock has been used by the Germans to such an extent that it is completely worn out. The Germans have not been able to fulfil their promise to supply enough coal. When the Quislings assumed power, one of their first moves was to tell the people that every housewife in the towns should have five hectolitres of coke to use during the coldest days of the year. But the effect of this promise was completely spoilt when the Norwegian broadcast from London informed the people that even this ridiculous little amount of coke was not German but British, and belonged to the legal Norwegian Government stores.

With regard to meat the situation is especially difficult in Northern Norway and in the big towns. In Oslo and some of the bigger towns there has been practically no meat or lard since before Christmas. In Oslo there are growing queues in front of the butchers from early in the morning to late in the afternoon to get hold of a small piece of meat. New restrictions upon what meat is in the market are being made every day. Those, however, who still had relations in the country were able to get some meat as late as February. Sausages do not exist any more, but an attempt has been made to substitute them with a fish sausage. The stores of whaling oil are now exhausted and most of the herring oil has been seized by the Germans. Commodities such as coffee—the consumption of which is very great in Norway—are practically impossible to get, because the Germans have confiscated the stores. A Norwegian now gets ten grams of coffee a week, while a German gets eighty. The same applies to tea, chocolate, and cocoa. Peas and peeled grain have completely disappeared, vegetables have been so expensive that few people can afford to buy them. The cakes which the German soldiers enjoyed so much, are now only a legend.

Since the beginning of December cellulose has been mixed with the flour. To begin with it was so little that it could hardly be tasted. In the middle of February, however, the amount of cellulose grew and the bread became blacker, softer, and heavier. This bread has undoubtedly already affected the health of the population, a proof of which is the increasing number of cases of stomach trouble.

It is now also clear that all grain will have been exhausted by April or May if the Germans do not keep their promise to return the 100,000 tons they 'borrowed' last year.

Butter and milk, on the other hand, have been available in sufficient quantities, but the milk production is decreasing and in many places milk is now rationed. There has also been enough sugar and potatoes and, if the Germans repay the 300,000 tons of potatoes they borrowed in 1940 the stock will last until the autumn. Cheese is very difficult to obtain. The lack of tobacco, which is increasing every week, has brought much suffering to smokers, and the story is told that two old sailors in Trondheim died of the lack of tobacco! The rationing of soap is very severe. Washing soap is not obtainable any more and the toilet soap is very scarce and of a poor quality. All sorts of substitutes are now on the market. Housekeeping in these days is extremely difficult, for rationing is very strict. It is a daily problem to know what to prepare for meals. 'You can't think of buying anything without a ration card, not even thread, yarn, or a tiny piece of cloth,' writes a Norwegian housewife in a letter to America. 'We get 300 coupons per year in our card, but a dress required 240 coupons, and a little yarn thirty coupons. A man can buy only one suit or overcoat a year. I am in despair when I think how many coupons it takes just to buy stockings for the boys.' Now also suits made from pulp are on sale in Norway as in Germany. Skins and hides have not been rationed, the reason being that the Germans want the Norwegians to make shoes and boots so that they can then take the best of them. There is still no real distress in Norway owing to the large reserve supplies, but the food situation is growing more and more dangerous, especially in the far north, and prospects for the winter are terrible. Norway has always been dependent on the import of grain for her food supplies during the winter; normally she produces between 15 and 20 per cent of the grain for bread.

A commodity which, so far, has not been lacking is money. The Germans at first paid very high wages for the work they wanted done on roads, aerodromes, barracks, and other military constructions. During the winter, however, there has been less work and also less pay. The very high rate of wages paid to begin with was a thinly disguised form of bribery, and many Norwegians fell for it. Recently, the Nazi-controlled 'Government' in Norway, on instructions from the German Reichskommissar, has started on a new line of policy with regard to prices. All prices must now be kept low by every possible means. It is obvious that this is leading to a subsequent lowering of wages, so that the Norwegian standard of living can be forced down to the Central European level.

None of the promises given by the Germans with regard to private building have been kept. Reconstruction and rebuilding of the towns destroyed during the fighting—probably more during two months than in the four months' fighting in Finland—has not yet started because of the increasing lack of building materials and undoubtedly also because the Germans have used for their own purpose, or have taken out of the country, timber and other raw materials. Timber is now being rationed.

Money has been made by owners of forest land, timber, merchants, carpenters, and building contractors; but for them, also, the prosperous days now seem to be on the wane.

On the other hand the difficulties for trade in general and for many industries, especially for textile manufacturers, have been constantly increasing because of the lack of raw materials and, not least, the lack of coal. The Germans have been unable to fulfil their promises to supply Norway with coal. Up to March they had only delivered 10 per cent of the amount of coal they had agreed upon.

The paper industry, for example, has had to close down owing to coal shortage, although activity in the pulp industry has continued on account of the growing demand for cellulose as cattle fodder. As a result, there is growing unemployment and short-time working. This applies also to the soap, oil, and fat industries, and to the match industry (which is working only thirty-eight hours a week). Other industries such as cement and rubber works are working short time. Everybody connected with shipping has been up against hard times, as nearly 90 per cent of the Norwegian Merchant Fleet is being employed outside Norwegian and German waters.

It is becoming more and more clear that all the German promises that Norway would remain an independent country within the German 'Lebensraum' have long been forgotten. Norway is treated as a German economic colony which now has to specialize in the production of raw materials, thus taking its place in the German economic system. The shipping fleet will never return to its pre-war size. Hamburg and Bremen, whose fleets, it is said, decreased after the first World War, must take over most of the transport and again become the transshipment ports for the northern countries. It is the revival of the old idea of supremacy, dating from the days of the Hanseatic League. All industries of no value to Germany are to be allowed to die, and other industries which are of special importance to the Germans are being taken over by German interests. This is particularly the case with regard to the exploitation of Norwegian water power and the chemical industries connected with the utilization of this power.

The Norwegians are forbidden to start new industries without permission from the Germans. Even big industrial undertakings which were planned in every detail, and on which work had actually begun, have been stopped. This was the case, for example, in connection with the erection of Norwegian iron works. These plans were stopped because the Germans decided to build a great aluminium works on the site. A German concern, the *Deutsche Mineraloelgeselschaft*, has taken over the Norwegian electro-chemical aluminium factories at Höyanger and Holmestrand, and the concern has also decided to use for new aluminium works other power stations, among the biggest in Norway, which are in the course of construction at the Tyin and Glomfjord waterfalls. German industry is thus taking over full control of these most important Norwegian power stations and industries. All work in connection with the building of the new factories will be carried out under German supervision and German machinery will be supplied.

Another big German concern, the *Hochtiefgeselschaft* in Berlin, has at the same time taken over the big power station at Aura, which is also under construction and which will likewise be used for the production of aluminium for Germany.

It is also supposed that the electrical power from these huge new power stations will be transferred by cable to Germany and thus provide material for the German war machine. It is significant that the Herman Goering Works (*Herman Goeringwerke*) constantly obtain more and more concessions, and that German engineers and administrative leaders are being put into all the important Norwegian business concerns in increasing numbers. In any case, the Norwegian Concession Laws, by which past Norwegian Governments have safeguarded Norway's natural resources from expropriation by foreign capital, have now been completely abrogated by order of the German Reichskommissar. During the last days of June, 1941, the Germans also tried to gain control of the Norwegian canning industry by appointing a German manager of the world-famous Stavanger firm Christian Bjelland and Company, Norway's greatest producers of canned food. Two weeks later they arrested the firm's senior partner, Consul Ragnvald Bjelland. This action constitutes one of the most open moves of the Germans to gain control over an important Norwegian industry, as they have done in all other occupied countries. As Norway depended more on foreign trade than most of the European countries, the economic life of the country has deteriorated considerably since the German occupation.

At the same time, as the Germans are doing their best to strangle Norway's economic life in favour of their own special interests; they do not mind extorting tremendous sums from the Norwegian population for maintaining the German army in Norway. The cost of the German occupation up to the end of February this year was something like £68,000,000 sterling—equivalent to £25 per head of the population. This does not include, of course, the goods and commodities that the Germans have taken out of the country, the value of which is estimated at about £28,000,000. In August one of the German officials from the Reichskommissariat told the member of the Administrative Council who was responsible for the finance of Norway, that in the next Norwegian budget an amount should be allotted for pensions for the families of German soldiers killed in Norway. The Norwegian, who was extremely brilliant, courageous, and outspoken, and therefore highly respected by the Germans, replied that the Administrative Council would consider the matter. 'It cannot,' he said, 'be a great amount, because your Fuehrer has told us officially that he lost only 1,300 soldiers in Norway, and not all of them were married. It cannot be a question of more than 700 to 800 soldiers.' The German official was quite unable to reply to this. He certainly knew that the Germans had lost 60,000 to 70,000 men in the Norwegian campaign, and he was therefore forced to drop the matter and it was never mentioned again!

Norway's exports to Germany are paid for in blocked marks, and Germany's account with Norway is steadily increasing. German soldiers' allowances in Norway are paid in Norwegian exchange drawn on the German account at the Bank of Norway. With this money they buy Norwegian products and send them to Germany. The establishment of a central clearing house in Berlin, which has accumulated large Norwegian balances in block marks, reveals the Nazi scheme to regulate the imports and exports not only of Norway, but of the whole continent. German purchases of foodstuffs and raw materials in Norway are, as already stated, also paid for out of this account. The consequences are, as we have seen, food shortage, acute shortage of raw material, and a steadily growing decrease in the value of Norwegian money.

CHAPTER 7

The Fight on the Home Front

FOR the overwhelming majority of the people it is quite clear that the National Union functions only as a tool of the occupation power. Even the Germans have been surprised to find how completely they have failed to convince their so-called Nordic brethren of their 'protection', and of the future happiness of the Norwegians in the German 'Lebensraum'.

Müller-Scheld, the chief censor responsible for the theatre, made an astonishing speech in the foyer of the National Theatre in Oslo when he welcomed a troop of German guest players. He said: 'You have come to a very highly cultured country, but 98 per cent of the population is pro-British. You have to win these people over with your art. From here you are going farther, to Bergen, where 150 per cent are pro-British!' However, the Germans failed in their artistic campaign, because nobody would go to the theatre, unless they were invited and could not refuse to attend. For instance, when the Hamburg Opera Company played at the National Theatre in Oslo, all the actors there were informed by the manager of the theatre that the Germans expected them to be present. One of the actors then telephoned to the Quisling Kommissar of Police and said to him that it surely would not be possible that they would all be forced to be present at the performance of the Opera Company. Many of the actors were going away for the week-end, he said, some had other things to do, etc. The Kommissar replied that, of course, the actors were free to do what they liked, but they should not do it as a demonstration against the Germans. The manager of the theatre, who was forced to be present on this occasion, then agreed that the actors who wanted tickets should sign their names on a list. Only the manager and a German-born hairdresser, attached to the theatre, signed the list!

The broad united political front which had been formed during the summer, became still more solidly united after Quisling came into power. All differences of opinion were buried. The old class and party spirit was dead. And after a few months the distinction between the Quislings and the real Norwegians was as clean-cut as if the division had been made with a sharp knife. You simply had to take a firm stand for or against Quisling. Even people who said they were not interested in politics were regarded as traitors if they did not finally admit that they were anti-Quisling. Now people loathe the very name of Quisling. There has been no revolution in Norway, and his meagre following of 2 per cent in 1936 has not grown; on the contrary, many people who for different reasons joined him after the 25th September, have since tried to back out when they became aware of the German plan to make Norway a German protectorate. The Quisling party was often joined by small business men, struggling to make a bare livelihood, badly paid employees, and unemployed workers, and this was mostly in the eastern part of the country. Wealthy farmers joined the movement, partly because they were strongly against the Communists and believed that the Quislings would protect the country from Communism, and partly because they believed that the Nasjonal Samling was the only institution by means of which Norway could obtain full national liberty and independence. At that time they really believed that Germany was going to win the war, but when they discovered that the Nasjonal Samling was only a messenger boy for the Germans, and when the Nazis began to requisition many thousands of their horses, their hay, and even searched for hay in the *Säters* (small farm huts, high in the mountains, where cattle are kept and a small amount of butter and cheese is produced), they became furious and many of them resigned their membership.

Quisling's new order is simply an order, created and supported and enforced by the German military and the Gestapo for the benefit of the conqueror and his plans. If left to themselves, as I have said, they would not continue for a day. Even Quisling himself has publicly admitted that the overwhelming majority is against him: 'That doesn't matter,' he says, 'Christianity was forced upon the Norwegian people by the old Viking Kings, and now I will do the same thing with the new order.'

There is little danger of conversions being made by propaganda, for the Norwegian front is now completely formed; but there is danger in the application of economic pressure which is being brought to bear on the individual and his family. Up till now very few people have given way under the pressure, and if they have been forced to join the Nasjonal Samling this has only served to increase their hatred of the 'new order'.

All over the country there have been many serious demonstrations against Quisling and his followers. Very few would listen to his speeches. In Bergen he was met by several thousand people who shouted: 'Down with the traitor,' and sang the National Anthem and 'God save the King'. Some people were so badly beaten that they had to be taken to hospital. The same thing happened in Trondheim where the Stormtroopers were beaten by the public and the German police had to rescue them. All over Norway the same thing happened. In Moss a loud speaker was blown up with dynamite and a lecture hall was stoned. The Constituted Ministers were received in the same way, especially the Minister of Police, Jonas (Judas) Lie, who had declared so many times that he was no Quisling. The Kommissar for propaganda, Mr. Gulbrand Lunde, recently visited a large factory to make a speech to the assembled employees. But instead of taking their places in the meeting hall, the workmen stood outside the door and greeted Lunde with a barrage of hoots and cat-calls. In fact the crowd was in such an angry mood that the Kommissar beat a hasty retreat to the Director's office without uttering a word! On another occasion, when a large propaganda meeting was scheduled for the employees of an iron foundry in Drammen, the workers obediently took their seats long before the arrival of the speakers. But when all was supposedly ready and the doors were thrown open for the grand entrance of the Nazi lecturers, not a single member of the audience was to be seen. The workmen had all slipped out the back-way, leaving behind them, as an audience, two disconsolate black cats!

There were, of course, acts of sabotage throughout the winter. In several cities sentences were imposed upon people accused of insulting German guards. A train was derailed. The Oslo–Bergen railroad was broken in ten places during very bad weather. The Germans said that the damage was due to natural causes, but at the same time a number of arrests were made. Electric cables running to anti-aircraft batteries and searchlights were cut. In Stavanger, Haugesund, and the surrounding districts, many German cables were cut during the winter, but the Germans were unable to discover the culprits. Then Terboven decreed on 9th April that the two towns and districts, in addition to a German fine of 70,000 crowns, must pay a contribution of 500,000 crowns. However, the sabotage is not yet of great value because the Germans can take horrible reprisals; but the population will wait for the great opportunity to arrive, when Germany is broken.

Characteristic of the feelings of the people in Bergen in Spring, 1941, is the story of a woman farmer who came to the market in Bergen with a basket of eggs. She sold only five eggs to each customer. A German came back and asked for five more eggs, but she refused to give him any more. Then a policeman arrived and promised the German that he would arrange it for him. 'No,' said the woman, 'if there is anything to be arranged I will do it myself,' and with that she put her foot down with full force, right in the middle of the basket of eggs, and went away. The story also tells how a man from Bergen, who witnessed the little scene, handed the woman a banknote in expression of his admiration. One day, in Bergen, a small boy was sitting in the street, weeping. A German passed by and, seeing him crying, gave him 5 öre (about a halfpenny) which the small boy, forgetting his tears in his fury, promptly hurled after the German with all his force. In the German section of the Haukeland hospital in Bergen a picture of Hitler was destroyed and the hospital was fined 1,000 kroner.

So far we have mostly undertaken passive resistance, centred around the King, who is now more popular and more beloved than ever. The singing of the Royal Anthem is forbidden and also the sale of pictures of the King and the Royal Family, but in every Norwegian home there is now a picture of the King. Emblems bearing the Royal Norwegian arms, or the Norwegian flag were worn by everybody until it was forbidden to do so. Then the public brought out ordinary Norwegian copper coins engraved with the initials of King Haakon and his motto: "Alt far Norge" (Everything for Norway) and used these as medallions until it was forbidden by law to 'wear Norwegian coins in sight'. Everywhere demonstrations took place in favour of the King, and it was impossible for the Germans and the Quislings to stop people from singing the National Anthem.

At the New Year celebrations at the Hotel Britannia, in Trondheim, at which many German officers were present, a very well-known actor arose at midnight and proposed a toast to the health 'of the noblest family in the country, who were terribly missed'. The whole of the assembled company, including the Germans, who were completely unconscious of the meaning of the toast, rose and cheered with tremendous enthusiasm. Afterwards the actor was arrested and he is now in prison.

On many of the blacked-out windows people have written: 'Long live the King.' On one window was written: 'Down with Quislings, dear King come back again soon.' Even in the snow the name of the King was to be seen everywhere, and along the ski tracks in the big forests around Oslo 'Long live the King' was written like a continuously unfolding band of ribbon.

A Norwegian who has recently escaped from Norway tells the following touching story:—

One day his little nine-year-old daughter came back from school and told him that during the Scripture class the door of the classroom had been opened just a crack and a hand, holding a placard on which was written: 'Long live the King,' appeared round the edge. 'Was it a big or a little hand?' he asked her. 'I can't tell you,' the little girl replied, 'because we have all promised to say nothing about it, but I can only say that it was a very long time before the teacher went out to see who was in the corridor!'

Even after the Quislings came into power and life became very difficult, the people did not forget how to laugh, and the most amusing stories, some of which are impossible to translate, were told everywhere and stimulated the resistance. One story which was to be heard all over the place, a few days after Quisling came into power, was the following: 'Have you heard the latest news? Quisling has taken over the tramways.' 'Why?' 'It's the only way he can get any more hangers-on!'

I do not vouch for the veracity of the next little story, but it is a good example of Norwegian humour:—

The inhabitants of a small fishing village in one of the fjords of Western Norway recently witnessed the forced landing of an airplane a few hundred yards from shore. One of the local fishermen set out by rowboat to rescue two pilots who were floundering in the water.

A crowd on shore watched the fishermen pick up the two airmen and start for land. But suddenly he pulled his oars in, grappled with the two men and threw them overboard. When he reached shore the sheriff questioned him:

'Why in blazes did you throw those men into the fjord?'

'They turned out to be Germans. I first thought they were British.'

'But did you drown them? Weren't they alive when you tossed them overboard?'

'Well, one of them said he was alive, but you know how these Nazis lie. . . .'

On the anniversary of the 9th April all over Norway people demonstrated against the Germans by staying at home from 2–2.30 p.m. In a leaflet distributed beforehand, the Norwegians were called upon not to appear in the streets or on the roads during this half-hour. 'Don't appear on the streets or visit restaurants or other public places. Shops and trains and trams shall be empty during this half-hour, which is dedicated to the memory of our fallen soldiers. House-wives: don't buy anything during this half-hour. Remain at home and take care that your children do the same. Business-men and clerks: don't use the telephone and don't answer it during this half-hour. Don't sell to people who dare to break this silence and in this way disgrace the memory of our warriors. Schoolchildren: in this half-hour don't answer any questions which your teacher may dare to ask you; sit quiet and look straight at members of the Hird, if there should be any in the classroom. Workers: do what you can to take part in the activity. Stand by the windows and be quiet, our own representatives will control the situation. No one should go out except to make sure that everything is quiet. It will certainly be quiet.' The letter ended in the following way: 'In this half-hour the wind could easily upset flower bowls on the heads of people who appear in the streets. Remember what we want and stand firm.'

The Quislings tried to disturb the demonstration and all of them appeared in the main street in Oslo, walking up and down, but all the other streets and roads were completely empty. In important factories the workmen went on strike and in the department offices and all public offices the employees remained idle. The heads of the largest Insurance company in Norway were summoned to appear before one of the Norwegian Kommissars, an insurance expert, who had been informed of what took place during this half-hour on 9th April by spies in the business belonging to the Nasjonal Samling. He threatened them but dared not proceed against them.

On 17th May, 1941, all national demonstrations and celebrations were forbidden—in Bergen even parties were forbidden. Many people were arrested all over Norway. In Bergen, for instance, all the main streets and open places were filled with marching Norwegians, since they were not allowed to stand still. They all wore rosettes and streamers in the national colours, and when the Storm Troopers attempted to remove these, the Norwegians hit back and some were arrested. When on several occasions throughout the day

British planes appeared overhead, the crowds hailed the Royal Air Force with tremendous enthusiasm, even in face of the German soldiers, who were at a loss to know what to do.

The most touching demonstration on this day took place when class after class of school children marched to the Möllendal Cemetery and placed wreaths on the graves of British airmen who lost their lives defending Norway. The wreaths bore inscriptions thanking the British airmen for what they had done for Norway. So many flowers were brought, that finally the white crosses themselves were completely covered.

At the Haukeland cemetery in Bergen the graves of thirteen British airmen are continually decked with flowers. The cemetery is just opposite the Haukeland school, now used as a barracks for German soldiers, and so the Nazis may witness daily from their windows the spectacle of Norwegian children bringing flowers to honour their British Allies. Even in winter when there is thick snow on the ground, every day there are fresh tracks to be seen around the graves. On twelve of the graves there are names, but in the thirteenth rests an unknown airman; to this grave the tributes of admiration and gratitude are brought in the highest number, here the greatest profusion of flowers is always to be found. And not only flowers are laid upon the graves, many people express their feelings by placing photographs and letters amongst the blossoms.

Parallel with the increase of German and Quisling pressure, grew the people's longing for Norwegian and British bombardment. The people became more and more dissatisfied, especially on the eastern side of Norway, where they did not even see the R.A.F. For instance, in a letter sent from a Norwegian town on the southern coast, at the end of May, the writer said: 'Sometimes we have a feeling that we are completely forgotten here in the mountains, but last week we were awakened by a terrific thundering sound, followed by a bang. We jumped out of bed and ran to the windows. Outside people were racing down the streets, and a fire-engine was rushing along at top speed. We opened the window a crack

(*Above*) The grave of an unknown British pilot.   Above it flies the Norwegian flag. Fresh flowers are placed on the grave every day.

(*Below*) Vidkun Quisling in an interview in front of the Ministry of Defence, February, 1932.

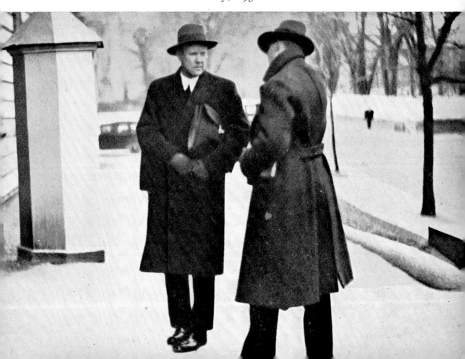

(*Above*) A German anti-aircraft gun and crew outside Oslo.

NORWAY'S OPPRESSORS

(*Below*) German officers leaving the command headquarters of the German Air Force at Oslo Airport.

Fliegerhorst
Kdtr. Oslo
Fornebu

and asked what was happening—the great benzine tank had just been bombed. Mr. X then dressed hurriedly and ran out to get some more news and to listen to what the people had to say about the great event. He came back and reported that the tank really had been bombed. The crowd was so excited and enthusiastic that they shouted "Hurrah" and there was a real 17th May feeling in the air. The streets were absolutely packed, but the next day there was not a single word about the incident in the newspaper—all such things must be hushed up. But it was a wonderful feat that the British, from the air, should have hit their target so accurately and exactly.'

Typical of public opinion in Oslo now is the remark made by an Oslo workman, some time ago: 'Let them bomb Oslo to pieces, let us hunger, let us be arrested, it's all the same if we can only get this damned devilry out of the country!' In Bergen, a crowd of children marched through the streets on the outskirts of the town, carrying a banner bearing the inscription: 'We demand more Air Raid Warnings!'

There is no section of Norwegian society—from tiny children to the aged and infirm—which is not actively and whole-heartedly taking part in the resistance to Nazi tyranny.

Under the leadership of the Supreme Court the fight for freedom and right was organized. The fact that the Norwegian Supreme Court resigned on 12th December made a tremendous impression. From the beginning, this Court had taken the lead in the fight for freedom and justice. The specific reason for their resignation was the Justice Department's decree of 14th November, whereby the departmental chief was given authority to discharge and appoint jurors, judges, and Court clerks, and also the fact that a judge of the Supreme Court, Mr. Emil Stang, was arrested without any form of trial. The Supreme Court asserted that the Justice Department's decree constituted an attack on law and order which was in open conflict with the recognized principles of justice, and would lead to the most fatal consequences, since the freedom of the Courts, which was guaranteed by the Constitution, was of vital importance to security and justice.

This decree violated the fundamental principles of Norwegian law, though both Hitler's decree of 24th April and the Reichskommissar's of 28th September had stated that the judicial system of Norway should continue to function as before, subject to the exigencies of the occupation. It was also contrary to article 43 of the Hague Convention of 1907, under which the laws of an occupied country should be respected by the invading power. In the correspondence entered into with Reichskommissar Terboven in this connection, a letter from Terboven stated that the Supreme Court had no authority to express its opinions on matters which had been dealt with by the Reichskommissar himself, or by any of the Norwegian so-called Constituted Kommissars. The validity of such decrees and orders could not be tested by the Supreme Court, or by any other Court in Norway. In conclusion he declared that the attitude of the Supreme Court was not to interfere with the political development. This statement confirmed the complete absence of all justice, and therefore all the judges of the Supreme Court refused to officiate any longer.

The Nazis were furious about this clear expression of opposition to the encroachment of the alien rulers upon the constituted law of Norway. They arrested the Chief Justice and one of the judges, but then the Bishop of Oslo intervened and they were set free. A new Supreme Court has now been formed, composed of second- or third-rate lawyers who support the Nasjonal Samling. This Court accepted the decree issued by the Quisling Minister of Justice, that it was not entitled to test the legal validity of decrees issued by Reichskommissar Terboven, or by government departments. Paragraph 43 of the Hague Convention has, therefore, been set aside by the Nazis.

The whole body of Norwegian lawyers, through the Central Committee of their National Association, then followed the Norwegian Supreme Court and the Norwegian Bishops in making a vigorous open protest against Quisling's violation of the basic principles of Norwegian law.

The Lawyers' Association condemned in particular various

decrees issued by the Quisling Ministries of Police and
Justice, especially dealing with the so-called People's Court.
They stated that the court is really a political one, because all
the judges belong to the Nasjonal Samling, and they constitute
a majority over the laymen attached to the court. This was a
direct violation of Norwegian law, which lays down that in all
cases falling within the scope of the penal code, the question
of 'guilty' or 'not guilty' must be decided by laymen. The
Public Prosecutor, who is a member of the Nasjonal Samling,
the former occupant of this position having been 'retired'
by the lowering of the age limit, has alone the power to decide
whether a case is brought before the People's Court or not.

The letter from the Central Committee of the Lawyers'
Association described all these arrangements as 'contrary to
the conditions which must exist in a state based on law'. The
letter also pointed out that many other decrees violate the basic
principles of Norwegian law, and that the principle of Habeas
Corpus is no longer respected. The signatories described the
new arrangement as causing great uneasiness and uncertainty
amongst the Norwegian people.

In January the State Church of Norway took up a
courageous and significant stand against the 'new order'. In
June, 1940, Terboven had given an assurance that the
guarantee of religious freedom, laid down in paragraph 46 of
the Hague Convention on Land Warfare, would be respected.
In consequence of this the Norwegian Bishops advised the
members of the Norwegian State Church to respect the
authority of the law, in accordance with the constitutional
position of the Church in the Norwegian State. On 15th
January, 1941, all seven Bishops of the Norwegian State
Church signed a letter [1] addressed to the Constituted Kommissar of the Department of Church and Education, in which
they demanded a clarification of the position of the Church
in German dominated Norway. 'The attitude of the Church,
needless to say,' wrote the Bishops, 'is at all times governed
by the basic principles outlined by Norway's Constitution, the

[1] For full text of the Bishops' letter, see Appendix 5, p. 147.

Articles of Faith and the Bible. It, therefore, is imperative and essential that the Church should know clearly whether the State, which is also concerned with ecclesiastical matters, accepts and honours the legal and moral obligations contained in the Church's Articles of Faith and the Bible.' They frankly indicted the present regime in Norway, accusing the puppet authorities of openly encouraging acts of violence and of contempt for the law. That the fundamental principles of Justice were being broken down, they stated, was shown by the following three concrete examples:—

(1) The systematic rule of terror by the Nazi Stormtroopers, an outstanding example of which was the attack on the Oslo Business College, on 30th November, during which teachers and the director were knocked down and severely assaulted. This was in itself bad enough, they said, but the seriousness of the event was increased by the slogan published that very morning by the official organ of the Quisling party: 'We shall strike again in such a way that they shall lose both sight and hearing. Stormtroopers, close your ranks. He who hits us once shall be hit tenfold. This shall be our watchword.' In addition to this there was the circular sent out by the Department of the Interior, of 16th December, in which all State and Municipal employees are ordered actively to support the Stormtroopers, and a refusal to do so would be looked upon as an action "inimical to the State" and would give rise to "drastic punishment". 'If such things,' the Bishops said, 'should continue systematically, the Church's servants would feel the lack of any basis for guiding the conscience of the people, in so far as respect and confidence in the law of the land were concerned.'

(2) The Resignation of the Supreme Court of Norway. 'The very fact,' the Bishops said, 'that all members of the highest court in the land have found it necessary to resign their duties is one that must create within the church a far-reaching feeling of insecurity with regard to the foundations of law and order in society.'

(3) Interference with the ministers' pledge of silence. 'To abolish this "Magna Charta" of the conscience,' the

Bishops said, 'is an attack upon the very heart of the Church.'

When they received an unsatisfactory reply to this request, the Bishops incorporated this answer and their reply in a circular letter to all the congregations of the Church of Norway, early in February, in which they repeated their previous charges that the Nazi regime was both lawless and Godless. 'When the authorities,' they said, 'permit acts of violence and injustice and exert pressure on our souls, then the Church becomes the defender of the people's conscience. One single human soul is worth more than the entire world.' They stated that the Church can never be silenced and they besought the authorities to strike out all that was against God's Holy Writ concerning justice, truth, and freedom of conscience and to build only upon the divine laws of life. At the same time, they besought the Norwegian people to avoid any use of force. 'He who promotes hatred or encourages evil will be judged by God.' 'The Holy Bible says: do not repay evil with evil but overcome evil with good, for above all of us stands the One who is Lord of our souls.' They ended the letter with these words: 'In our congregations we now observe a ferment of conscience and we feel it our duty to let the authorities hear, clear and loud, the voice of the Church.'

All the Christian organizations of Norway, various denominations of the State Church, the Salvation Army, and the various Missions, joined in the stand taken by the Bishops. The Episcopal Letter was forbidden to be read aloud in the churches by the authorities, but many Ministers read it nevertheless, and the Circular Letter was distributed all over Norway causing the resistance to become stronger and stronger.

During this action the party of the Association of Ministers prepared a prayer for the Bishops to be read in the churches. On the 14th February the chairman of the Association received a telegram from the Kommissar of Church and Education forbidding the prayer to be read on Sunday, 16th February. But the party stood firm in its refusal to obey this command, and the result was that on Saturday, 15th

February, the Kommissar asked them to regard his telegram of 14th February as not having been sent, and the prayer was read in the churches all over the country the next day.

In March the Ministers decided to boycott the Nazi sermons given over the radio, and the Bishops, in a proclamation asked all the Ministers to support the boycott. All the Christian organizations called upon their members to join in this boycott and to refuse to co-operate with the broadcasting so long as the situation remained as it was.

The Germans in the last few months have been greatly worried by the courageous stand taken by the Bishop of Oslo, Mr. Berggrav, and there was a rumour that they had planned to arrest him. One of the German Kommissars asked a well-known Norwegian what the consequences of the arrest of the Bishop would be. The Norwegian replied that the next day there would be no Bishop in Norway. The German then said that one of the Deans could take over his authority, but the Norwegian answered that no Bishop would consecrate a Dean who was willing to take over this position after the Bishop was arrested. Then the German said that it would be possible to ask a Swedish Bishop to become the successor of Mr. Berggrav, but the Norwegian replied that such a possibility could only exist in the dreams of the Germans.

In February the schools in Oslo and the surrounding districts went on strike against the attempt to make the teaching of the Nazi ideology compulsory, and against the violent attacks made by Hirdmen on loyal scholars. An outstanding example of Hird brutality is the case of a 13-year-old boy who was given fifteen stripes with a leather strap on his bare body because of his alleged anti-Nazi behaviour.

When the Nazi authorities ordered the schoolchildren to visit the Hitler Jugends Exhibition, the overwhelming majority of the children refused to do so, and even quite young children demonstrated in the streets of Oslo, shouting: 'Down with Quisling,' 'Long live the King,' outside the German headquarters, and singing the National Anthem outside the empty royal palace. The police attempted several times to disperse them, but no sooner had a demonstration been broken up in one street, than it reopened in another. The constituted Kommissar for Church and Education then repeated the order and threatened to close the schools if the order was not obeyed. However, this only resulted in five rectors visiting the Exhibition, and very few children followed their example—in one case two, the highest number being twenty. From many High Schools no teacher or pupil appeared at the Exhibition at all. School strikes have also been declared in Bergen and other places, and the Quisling authorities and the police, on behalf of the Germans, have threatened the schools with the most serious consequences. For example, the Germans told the rectors of the schools in Oslo and Aker that if the schools were not opened again by 12th February the Germans would occupy them and use them as barracks. The rectors then decided that the schools should reopen, but at the same time, asked for a guarantee that they would be left to work in peace.

Just before Easter a school strike broke out in a high school in the neighbourhood of Oslo, the reason being that the pupils in one of the classes refused to greet the newly appointed Quisling rector when he entered the classroom. When the rector turned the pupils of that class out of the school, their comrades in all the other classes made a common stand and refused to go to school, too. The Quisling authorities then asked for a declaration of loyalty from the parents, on behalf of the pupils, but they were refused. The school then had to be reopened without any compromise having been made either by the pupils or their parents, and the position of the new rector had suffered terribly. The problem is not yet solved, and it certainly never will be so long as the Quislings and the Germans are in Norway.

Town and County Councillors and Municipal Government officials are refusing in large numbers to accept the dictates of the Quislings. The strong tradition of local self-government in Norway is a serious obstacle to the dictatorial centralization which the Nazis are seeking to impose. Hundreds of local Councillors and officials, who have been instructed to carry out the decrees issued by the Kommissars of Justice, Police, and Propaganda, without regard to the Norwegian municipal laws or the Constitution, have resigned in protest, and many have been arrested and imprisoned.

In Bergen the four thousand State and municipal employees refused to take an active part in the work of the Nasjonal Samling, as they had been ordered to do by the Constituted Minister for the Interior. Only fifteen officials, who were already members, agreed to obey the new order.

In Aker, the surrounding district of Oslo, fifty municipal employees, who refused to greet the new Chairman of the local council, were suspended for fourteen days without pay. Then other employees protested and declared that they would go on strike if this order were not repealed.

The Quisling Civil Service, like the German Civil Service, is thoroughly inefficient owing to the lack of experts and competent people on the staff. Many of the Quisling Civil Servants are utterly corrupt and the salaries they receive, compared with those paid to the former Norwegian Civil Servants, are fantastically high. Not only members of the Nasjonal Samling, but also their families and their friends were given appointments, many of which were specially created for them.

Since loyal Norwegians in every section of society refused to have anything to do with the Quislings, they were forced to call in third-rate adventurers and disgruntled careerists to take up responsible positions in central and local government departments.

Since the Reichskommissar's decree of 15th February, membership of the Nasjonal Samling, regardless of personal qualifications, has become the decisive factor in the appointment of officials of any kind. On 3rd April twenty-two powerful public and professional organizations protested against this decree, which was a flagrant breach of the Reichskommissar's promise that they would not be forced to join the Nasjonal Samling. They received no answer from Terboven.

Examples of the incapacity of the civil German administration in Norway are now becoming very numerous, but a few of them should be put on record. A very high official within the Norwegian administration one day received a visit from one of the members of the German administration who said that it was now necessary 'that the big fisheries should start at once'. He had no idea that the fisheries linked up with the seasons. He thought, apparently, that only a word of command from the Germans could bring the fishes to the Norwegian coast. It is also well known in the construction of barracks for the German soldiers incredible amounts were thrown away. In many places the work was suddenly stopped and all the materials became useless. Also with regard to most of the other works by the Germans, it is apparent that they were very badly planned and that they were stopped again and again by orders contradicting each other. Most of the members of the German administration were extremely ignorant and stupid, and all the Norwegians were simply flabbergasted by the stupidities which the young German Kommissars could commit. The chief of the German census in Norway, for example, had never heard of Fridtjof Nansen. The Chief of the Gestapo in Ålesund was searching the house of a barrister, outside the town. In the library he discovered a copy of a book by the famous Prussian philosopher, Immanuel Kant. 'Immanuel,' he exclaimed, 'who is this man? Immanuel must certainly be a Jew!' and he took the book away with him. A friend of mine, who was arrested, afterwards told me that the Gestapo was even more soulless and mechanical than he had imagined.

The explanation of this surprising phenomenon is that the Nazis have concentrated everything upon the war machine and war production. They have neglected their spiritual life, their schools, high schools, and universities. Those young people who have been given positions of authoritiy and power, have been chosen solely because they were members of the Nazi party, and not because of their ability. This outstanding difference between the Germans of the first World War and the second World War is the Achilles' heel of Germany.

At the same time that people must not underrate the Nazi war machine and their military efficiency, they must also not over-estimate their administrative ability.

Since I escaped from Norway I have heard the same thing about all occupied countries. A prominent Dane characterized the Nazi administration in Denmark as follows: 'Ordre, contraordre, désordre.' In France they were astonished that the Nazis were so stupid, incapable, and corrupt, and President Benes had similar reports about *his* country. The young fools brought from Germany and put into office were so ignorant of the most ordinary, elementary things that they just appeared incredibly stupid. They simply knew nothing. They were completely ignorant of national, cultural, and economic life. They were quite uneducated, and they often violently disagreed with each other. The German High Command was ignorant of the negotiations with the Storting in June, and became furious when told about it. The army was against the Kommissars, the civil police against the Gestapo, and within every branch different groups opposed each other. It was, therefore, very difficult to get a quick decision. It very often happened that an order was counter-manded the very next day. Already we then realized that the 'new order' was in reality only disorder, chaos, and confusion, that the Nazis could only destroy not create, and we said: 'If the Germans are a people of masters, as they tell us, then we, the Scandinavian democrats, must be superhuman.'

The secret of the new order was that it was only a myth, a new version of Anderson's Fairy Tale, about the Emperor's new clothes—everybody believed in these invisible clothes until a little child suddenly proclaimed the plain truth: 'Look, the Emperor is walking around without any clothes on.'

The growing unrest of all sections of the Norwegian people was again voiced by forty-three of the most prominent national organizations in Norway in a joint open letter on 15th May to the German Reichskommissar Terboven. The letter was signed by the leaders of organizations representing university profes sors, judges, clergymen, teachers, doctors, business men, civil servants, municipal employees, trade unionists, and all classes of professional, technical, administrative and industrial workers.

The letter stated that the indignation of the people has increased to a marked degree in the past weeks. It detailed a whole series of incidents resulting from the illegal and terroristic activities of Quisling's Nasjonal Samling Party and his band of stormtroopers. The signatories protested in particular against the brutalities committed by the Hird (Quisling's Black Guard) in schools and colleges and at public meetings, and against the kidnapping of Dr. Gjessing, the Director of the Dikemark Mental Hospital near Oslo.

They stated that the decrees issued by the Quisling Kommissars of Justice and Police are in open contradiction both to Norwegian law and international law, and that the doctrine of 'private retaliation', officially endorsed by the Quisling Public Prosecutor, exposes Norwegian citizens to brutal assaults without possibility of legal redress.

Civil servants and municipal employees, so the letter states, have been threatened with dismissal if they do not join the Nasjonal Samling, and vacant positions are filled with Nasjonal Samling people without any regard to their technical qualifications.

A letter from the Ministry of the Interior to the Administrative Office in Bergen, demanded that all municipal employees in Bergen should state in writing their views on (*a*) Vidkun Quisling, (*b*) the Nasjonal Samling, and (*c*) co-operation with the German occupation authorities. It is significant that out of 4,000 public employees in the Bergen district only twelve, under pressure, joined the Nasjonal Samling.

In conclusion the representative of the forty-three organizations stated that 'the overwhelming majority of Norwegians must regard these activities of the Nasjonal Samling as an attempt to force them to compromise with their consciences and abandon the path of duty'. And they demanded a reply to their letter.

After a visit from Himmler, Terboven struck. He suddenly

arrested many of the chairmen and representatives of the forty-three organizations, and the Kommissar for the Interior, Hagelin, dissolved all the scientific organizations.

On Wednesday, 18th June, all the people who had signed the famous letter of protest were summoned by Terboven to a meeting at the Storting House. After delivering a lecture Terboven called out the names of five of these people—very prominent people—and ordered them to come and stand before him, exactly like school children. He then informed them that they would have 'plenty of time in which to think over what they had done'. After this he ordered the German police to arrest them on the spot, thus forcing all the other people present to witness the scene. Then Hagelin spoke and said that he now had authority to dissolve all the organizations he wished.

Nazi 'controllers' (Treuhändlerne) were now appointed to take charge of the various organizations of trade unionists, civil servants, professional workers, and business men, which had sent the joint letter of protest to the Kommissar.

Terboven, exposing to an unprecedented degree his devilish mentality, got the 'controllers' on 3rd July to sign a proclamation on behalf of twenty-one of these organizations, begging the Norwegian people to send volunteers to fight against Russia in Finland. This outrageous insult has aroused a blazing fury in all circles in Norway. The labourers and workers are especially incensed because the representative of the Trades Union Congress was one of the five men arrested in the Storting building.

Quisling has failed either to build up any following amongst the people of Norway or to establish a competent civil administration. Considering the fact that the Quislings have had at their disposal, for many months, all the tools of propaganda and all the governmental machinery, thousands of Gestapo, and hundreds of thousands of German troops, it is astounding how little they have been able to influence the Norwegian people. More and more the Germans have been forced to intervene in an attempt to clear up the resulting confusion. Now, apparently, they intend to take things into their own hands entirely. Terboven's proclamation of the 26th March, which established the death penalty for a long series of offences, which I have mentioned before, is amongst the measures which, in fact, amount to complete German military and political control of Norway. These offences are to be tried by German military courts; thus, without any formal declaration of Martial Law, the Germans have imposed an iron military dictatorship on Norway, and put the Quisling Council of Kommissars under their 'protection'.

All the former promises of both Terboven and Quisling, to preserve the independence of Norway and to respect Norwegian law in the internal administration of the country, have been thrown aside. One of the reasons for the decree of Terboven, establishing martial law in Norway, was that the resistance of the people was beginning to have an effect upon the morale of the German soldiers in Norway.

The morale of the German army began to decline during the winter. The soldiers were longing for home, and many of them, especially the older ones, were influenced by our former peaceful democratic life and by our stubborn resistance.

Some girls, unfortunately, fraternized with the German soldiers, to the fury of the young Norwegian men, who tried every way of demonstrating against this, and in many cases were arrested. But the great bulk of the population cold-shouldered the Germans, and many Germans really suffered mentally in this ice-cold atmosphere. A German officer, who had taken part in the fighting in Poland, said that it was bad enough to see the furious hatred in the eyes of the Poles, but it was even worse to face the cold contempt of the Norwegians. And when the invasion of Germans steadily increased and they descended like a swarm of locusts, eating up all that the land could offer, the relations between the civil population and the German army became more and more strained.

The Germans had between three to four hundred thousand troops in Norway, some for the occupation of the country, some of them intended for the invasion of England, others, in the far north, as a guard against Russia, but many of them, in the valleys and places of no strategic importance, were on a fattening campaign, and when their belts were tight they were replaced by fresh troops, who regarded Norway as a sanatorium. In the first months, the German soldiers had generally behaved very well, and there were few clashes between the Germans and the civil population. Therefore it was with some surprise that, after 15th September, I frequently saw completely drunken German soldiers lurching down the main streets of Oslo, about one or two o'clock in the afternoon. And when the autumn came, with dark afternoons and long nights, and the whole country—with the exception of the brilliantly lighted German barracks at Skougum, and the residence of Terboven—was blacked out, terrible stories about the kidnapping of young girls, and even of murder, were reported everywhere. Many of these rumours were exaggerated, but a few terrible tragedies did occur. The younger soldiers were still all for Hitler, and very enthusiastic, but many of the older ones, even officers, openly admitted—when they trusted the Norwegians in whose house they were billeted—that they were strongly opposed to this war, and that they hoped to get rid of Hitler.

In a letter of January, 1941, smuggled out of Norway, the writer said of the German soldiers that they were a mixture of good and evil, like everything else in life. 'Some of them,' the writer said, 'were very good people, but all of them have this in common—they are very childish, and quite five years younger, in every way, than Norwegians of their own age.

'In the beginning it was hopeless to enter into a political discussion with them, because everything was arranged by Hitler, and peace would come on 15th August! Their political ignorance was incomprehensible. Most of the troops returned to the Ruhr and the Rhineland for a vacation of three weeks, and when they came back to Norway they were very much changed. From then on they were very anxious to hear the latest news, and to discuss the possibilities of victory or defeat. My impression was that some of them would like to make the peace to-morrow—at any price. One evening in November a German came into the house and I asked him if he was permitted to listen to the broadcasts from London. 'No,' he said, 'the penalty for that is two years in prison.' I then asked him if he would like to listen to the German news from London. At first he hesitated and then finally agreed to do so. After he had heard it he turned to me in astonishment and said: 'Is there really war in Albania?' He knew nothing about this. Such is their lack of knowledge!

In March, 1941, the young people who arrived in London from the Lofoten Islands, told us that many of the German soldiers who had been taken prisoner and conducted to England on this occasion, were very happy to be captured, because they were heartily sick of the war. These young people also told us that Austrian soldiers in Norway had said: 'If the British really come here we will not only surrender, but we will also join them.'

Although the morale of the German army did not actually reach breaking point, there were many signs that the soldiers in Norway had a different mentality from those in Germany. The Gestapo, therefore, tried to control them, and the relations between the Army and the Gestapo grew worse. The following story, which was told me by a very great friend, is a good illustration of these relations. My friend was sitting on the first floor in one of the big restaurants in Oslo, which was practically empty. There were some German officers at a table, and near them was a very Quisling looking Norwegian. The German officers were talking to each other when suddenly the Norwegian interrupted them, and said something to them. They listened to him for a while, then suddenly one of the officers stood up and shouted: 'Get out, you damned Gestapo.' The Norwegian became very confused and perplexed and stammered: 'I am Norwegian, I am not Gestapo,' but the officer simply replied: 'Get out, you bloody Gestapo.'

CHAPTER 8

The Battle of Free Norway

FROM the very first day of the World War the Norwegian Merchant Fleet has taken part in it and has suffered greatly.

In the first World War the Norwegian Mercantile Marine sailed all the time, even when the Germans, in 1917, declared unlimited submarine war, and many neutrals kept their ships in harbour. We therefore suffered terrible losses, and at the end of the war we had lost nearly 49 per cent of the fleet, and 2,000 sailors.

As fourth amongst the world's seafaring nations, the Norwegian Merchant Fleet in this war is not only playing the same part as it played twenty-five years ago, but is also playing a role of far greater importance for the ultimate issue, especially in the battle of the Atlantic, than it did before. For the fleet is much more efficient than it was in the last war, and is probably more modern and better equipped than any other merchant fleet in the world, and is manned by really first-class crews, whose fame has been recognized on all the seas.

At the beginning of the war, in September, 1939, the Norwegian Merchant Fleet consisted of 1,990 vessels, amounting to 4,800,000 gross registered tons. The average age of a Norwegian ship was lower than in any other Merchant Fleet in the world. Two-thirds of the Norwegian vessels were driven by Diesel engines, with a speed of from 12 to 16 knots under full load, and had an annual carrying capacity 40 to 60 per cent in excess of the 10-knot steamer. Our tanker fleet of over two million tons, had an oil-carrying capacity nearly equal to that of the British tanker fleet. Even before the war by far the greater part of the Norwegian Merchant Fleet was engaged in international trade, and the tonnage engaged in ocean-going traffic exceeded that of the United States and

(*Above*) The Crown Prince inspects units of the Norwegian Air Force in Canada.

NORWAY'S WAR EFFORT

(*Below*) Officers and men of a Norwegian destroyer marching past the Crown Prince.

NORWAY'S GREATEST CONTRIBUTION TO THE ALLIED CAUSE
(*Above*) A merchant ship, manned by a Norwegian crew and their captain,
brings American planes safely to England.

GETTING READY TO HIT BACK AT THEIR ENEMY
(*Below*) Norwegian soldiers on manœuvres in Scotland.

Japan and was only surpassed by that of Britain. Already before Norway herself entered the war, a considerable part of the Norwegian fleet was in the service of the Allies, mainly by direct chartering to the Allied Governments.

During the period before the 9th April, fifty-four Norwegian ships were lost by war action, and 600 sailors were killed. When the Germans suddenly attacked Norway, on the 9th April, some Norwegian ships were in Norwegian ports and some also in Swedish ports. Some of them escaped and all the ships scattered over the high seas obeyed the Government. Not a single Norwegian ship in any part of the world not dominated by the Nazis obeyed the German orders, and they all went to Allied or neutral ports. Several other Norwegian ships escaped also from Italian ports. The Norwegian fleet at that time amounted to about a thousand ships, totalling more than four million tons, but is now (June, 1941) reduced to about 950 vessels totalling about 3,600,000 tons. The Norwegian Government immediately took steps to preserve the ships for the nation, and requisitioned them and transferred the control from private owners to the Norwegian State. The entire fleet is now administered by the Norwegian Shipping and Trade Mission, which is the largest shipping concern in the world. Its headquarters are in London. From now on further tonnage was placed at the disposal of the British Government, so that now far more than half of our fleet is sailing on routes which are of benefit to England and to our common war supplies. But the rest of the fleet is also engaged in work which directly serves the common cause. A very considerable quantity of oil, which is so valuable and so indispensable for the prosecution of the war, is carried in Norwegian tankers. 25,000 Norwegian sailors bring petrol, munitions, and foodstuffs to Great Britain and other theatres of the war. It was, therefore, with some reason that the *Motor Ship* in its issue for January, 1941, said: 'It is probably an understatement to say that at the present time this Fleet is worth more to us than a million soldiers.'

Many ships have been sunk by bombs and torpedoes. During the period from the beginning of the invasion until

February, 1941, more than 350,000 tons were lost—almost exactly the same as the losses during the seven months before the invasion. The loss of human life was actually less during this war period than before. At the end of 1940 the number of Norwegian sailors lost was 307, besides thirty-seven of other nationalities.

In January the losses were nineteen ships, 64,242 tons, and in February, eight ships, 27,002 tons. In January forty-two Norwegian sailors were lost and in February, eighty-nine.

In March the fleet lost sixteen ships, amounting to 63,000 gross registered tons; fifty-nine sailors were lost, and many are missing. In April eleven ships amounting to about 45,000 gross registered tons were lost and seventy sailors, with thirty-five missing.

I have had the opportunity to meet these sailors in many parts of the world. I have seen them in Japan, and in California. I have met people taken prisoner by raiders in the Indian Ocean. I have met thousands of sailors in the Eastern American ports and in Halifax. Since then I have met them in all the big ports in Great Britain. I have listened to their tales. I have heard about their sufferings in open lifeboats, fired at by German machine-guns. I have read reports of ships which have been given distinctions by the British Admiralty. Many Norwegians have valiantly defended their ships, fighting with machine-guns against hell-fire of bombs of all types, rained down on them from the German planes, and some have even succeeded in bringing down German planes. On one occasion, two German planes were brought down by one ship alone. These feats, their magnificent fighting in the battle of the Atlantic, certainly form one of the finest chapters in the Saga of Norway. They were never afraid. Men who were bombed or torpedoed went out again and again. The only thing they were really afraid of was that their families in Norway might starve, while they were bringing foodstuffs and other necessities to Great Britain. They were real heroes, but to them their deeds of heroism were simply part of the day's work.

Very characteristic is the following story which the Norwegian poet, Nordahl Grieg, tells:—

He visited in hospital a very young sailor who had been torpedoed, and, as the sole survivor from the ship, had been alone on a raft for eleven days in the North Atlantic. When he was rescued by British destroyers, he was so weak and so ill that it was feared at first that his legs would have to be amputated. When the boy had told Mr. Grieg his story he asked him where he came from. 'From London,' Mr. Grieg replied, and then the young sailor became filled with pity. 'Oh, no, no,' he said, 'it must be terrible to live there!'

Although the Norwegian freighter *Dokka* of Bergen sank within thirty seconds after being torpedoed by a German submarine in the Atlantic, members of the crew escaped drowning by clinging to two separate rafts which had broken loose from the sinking ship. As the survivors lay tossing about on the heavy seas the U-boat approached the second mate's raft and asked the name of the ship and its tonnage. Having obtained information about the tonnage but not about the name, the U-boat then approached the captain's raft and again asked the name of the sunken ship. The captain replied by giving them a false name, and then suddenly they saw a British escort destroyer approaching, and the German submarine swiftly disappeared. The Norwegians shouted to the destroyer which, after a while, came alongside the floating raft, but the Norwegians were not concerned with being rescued. 'Go after the U-boat first, we can wait,' they said. For eight hours the sailors waited in the wintry north Atlantic. Then the destroyer returned, having located and sunk the submarine, and rescued the patient Vikings. This is the spirit of the Norwegian sailors.

Thanks also to Norway's Merchant Marine, the Norwegian Government has financial resources which enable it to wage war for the liberation of Norway, to meet all its foreign obligations, in Allied and neutral countries, to build up a reserve for speedy provisioning and reconstruction when the Germans have been driven out of Norway, and to establish a sound financial system after the war.

When the King and the Government, on the 7th June, had to leave Norway they were resolved to continue the fight, and immediately after they arrived in London they set to work to organize the Norwegian forces. Thousands of sailors, whalers, and other Norwegians living outside the country, and also officers and soldiers who left Norway, have enlisted in the Army, Navy, and Air Force. They are constantly being joined by a steady stream of young men from occupied Norway, coming over in fishing craft and smacks, and even in rowing boats. The 300 young people who followed the British warships from the Lofoten raid, after only a few minutes in which to make their decision, tell more about the fighting spirit of the Norwegian youth than any words could do. Many others have had to cross the forests into Sweden and then journey through Russia and Siberia, or Iran, to Bombay or Capetown, to join the Royal Norwegian Air Force in Canada, and the most recent reports from Norway tell moving stories about the young people there who are longing to escape in order to be able to fight for their country, envying their comrades who have already succeeded in doing so. Some of the escaping boats disappear, but this does not frighten them; even the strictest and most vigilant German control, and the imposition of the death penalty for attempting to escape, are powerless to prevent Norwegians from escaping to join the forces of their legal Government. The German occupation has taught these young people that life is not worth living under the Nazi regime, and that no sacrifice is too great to regain their liberty, which is an indispensable condition of life.

An Army training camp was established in Scotland. The troops have been fully trained after several months, and supplied with all kinds of modern equipment. They form the nucleus of a Norwegian expeditionary force. A detachment from the camp in Scotland participated in the Anglo-Norwegian Lofoten expedition. Another detachment of the Norwegian Army was established in Iceland last autumn, and is now completely trained and ready for action.

The Norwegian Navy is steadily increasing, because most of the people temporarily stranded in Great Britain or coming over from the western coast of Norway are sailors and fishermen. A few Norwegian warships reached England after the Germans captured Northern Norway, and they have been in service since that time in co-operation with the British Navy. They include some small destroyers, submarines, armed trawlers, patrol boats, minesweepers and a number of torpedo boats which had been under construction in England. Four of the destroyers which America presented to Great Britain have been taken over by Norway and are manned and run under the Norwegian flag and command. One of these was employed in the raid on Öksfjord, in the north of Norway, but they are mostly used for convoy duties.

In Scotland and on the Canadian east coast recruiting and training camps have been established; here we have also armed and equipped a large number of Norwegian whaling vessels for official duties. There are about seventy of them in service and they are well known for their speed and for their ability to withstand practically all kinds of waters. They are acting as coastal patrols, convoy guards, and minesweepers. Some of them, for example, are serving in the West Indian waters, others are at Newfoundland, and many have been stationed in Iceland and farther south.

The new Norwegian Air Force was established in Canada as England could not spare aerodromes or material for the training, and as Norway had already placed orders in the United States for fighter and bomber training planes. Near Toronto an extensive training camp was built, called 'Little Norway', to which young Norwegians from all over the world have flocked. Both an Army air arm and an Air Force have been formed under single command. Some Norwegian planes were flown across to England from Norway last summer and participated in the war.

I have seen this camp in Toronto, which is a model of organization and efficiency and has aroused the admiration of every foreigner who has visited it. I have seen the training, and my heart has been warmed by the enthusiasm and the spirit of these young people, who are yearning to liberate their country and to pay the Germans back for what they have done to Norway. Norway to-day possesses an Air Force many times greater than the former Air Force in Norway, and soon it will be in action on this side of the Atlantic. I met the same spirit everywhere I went. I have visited the naval camp in Canada, I have met the young naval ratings in Scotland and in the British naval ports. I have talked to our sailors and our soldiers in Scotland—a section of whom are already on duty as coastguards. I have been proud to meet them, and my heart was warmed again when I felt their enthusiasm and witnessed their eagerness to train, to learn, to prepare for the great fight to come. I have never seen Norwegian forces—small as they are—of such standing and such quality.

For many of these sailors and whalers, who have now become soldiers, marching and exercising is a dull life. They are longing for a real fight, and in March some of them had the opportunity to deliver a blow to the Germans in Norway. The raid on Lofoten, planned by the British and Norwegian Royal Navies and executed by British ships with a detachment of Norwegian soldiers acting as guides, was a tremendous success. The Lofoten oil factories were destroyed, about 18,000 tons were sunk, over 200 Germans were taken prisoner together with a few Quislings, and more than 300 young Norwegian men and women who were longing to join the forces in Great Britain were taken back. The British and Norwegians suffered no losses in this raid. Before destroying the wireless station the Norwegian officers sent a telegram to Adolf Hitler in Berlin: 'You said in your latest speech that everywhere where British troops should land in Europe they would meet German soldiers. Here we are, but we haven't met your soldiers. We will be back again soon and hope to meet you.' This raid on Lofoten was of great importance as a warning to the German Army that it could not consider itself safe. Since that time many of the garrisons and troops on the western coast have been reinforced, and the Germans and their Quisling followers live in a constant state of fear and nervousness that they may be taken by surprise again. The raid aroused the greatest enthusiasm amongst the people of Norway, and they were delighted to learn that some of their own countrymen took part in the expedition by the side of their British allies. They hailed it as a token of Spring, but of course they understood that one swallow doesn't make a summer. They are still waiting and hoping for new expeditions, and many young people are waiting to join the raiders and cross the sea.

The next raid took place in April. This time Norwegian sailors and soldiers only took part, in an American destroyer. They destroyed an oil factory in Öksfjord. In spite of the fact that the raid was a success, the young Norwegians who took part in it were very disappointed that they did not come into direct contact with the German soldiers, and that they had no room on board to take any Norwegians back with them, for here again they found the people filled with the same enthusiasm and the will to sacrifice. They did, however, bring back with them a pair of hand-knitted mittens with the wrists bordered with the national colours and with the words: 'Long live the King' worked into the design. Even in the far north the love of freedom and loyalty to the King is as burning and fervent as in the far south.

The raid on Lofoten made the German Reichskommissar Terboven nearly mad with fury. He went at once by air to Lofoten and ordered the most severe reprisals, which only served to strengthen the resistance and increase the hatred of the people for the Nazis. Some people were shot and many were imprisoned. The Dean of Svolvær, a very highly esteemed man, and seventy other people from Lofoten from 70 to 17 years, were taken as hostages and sent to Oslo where they were interned in a new concentration camp in Hakadal, near Oslo. They were maltreated, prevented from sleeping at night and even refused water, and when they marched through Trondheim, on their way to the railway station, a very old man fell exhausted in the street—but the German soldiers, taking no notice, dragged him along by his feet to the station. In Oslo during the examination they had to stand completely motionless, and if they dared to make the slightest movement they were beaten until they fell unconscious to the ground. Ten of the houses belonging to the families of the young people who had left with the raiders were burnt as a punishment, and the inhabitants forced to watch the destruction of their homes. Neighbours were forbidden to house the destitute inhabitants for the first night. All the villages and towns were heavily fined. At once Norwegians everywhere organized a collection to pay the fines and the necessary sum was raised, but then the new Quisling Chief of Police in Lofoten decreed that no one but the inhabitants of the places which had been fined could pay the amount due. This act of wanton destruction and revenge, this brutal violation of international law, has caused bitter indignation throughout Norway, and the incident is taken as an indication of the Nazis' growing nervousness and fear for future raids.

To prevent young people from escaping from Norway, the Germans have forced the Norwegians living on the coast to leave their houses this summer, and have put German families from bombed cities into them. For example, in Aalesund and the surrounding districts they have, in a few weeks, arrested over forty fathers of young boys who have escaped to England, and have sent them to concentration camps in Hakadal.

On 25th June they went so far as to declare a state of siege in Bergen, and forbade all people to leave their homes from 9 p.m. until 5 a.m. During these hours of curfew all traffic must be stopped and civilians must stay in their houses. Civilians are expressly forbidden to lean out of their windows on the side facing the street. Severe penalties are imposed for disobeying these instructions.

It is interesting to note that the placards bearing these instructions, which were placed around the town, were not dated 25th June, 1941, but 12th September, 1940—one of the days the Germans had chosen for the invasion of Great Britain.

The Lofoten raid proved that the Norwegian people in occupied Norway are still spiritually with their King and Government and their Allies in the fight. The men and women from Lofoten not only told the true story about the feelings of the Norwegian people, but they also revealed the fact that the Germans have not succeeded in crushing the spirit of

(*Above*) General view of Stamsund, showing oil burning on the water after the oil tanks had been set ablaze.

LOFOTEN RAID

(*Below*) Some of the oil wells on fire after being detonated.

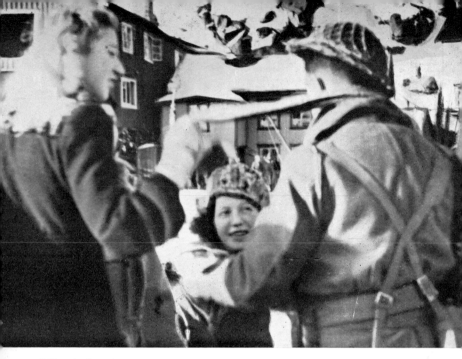

(*Above*) On the quayside. A Norwegian girl takes a soldier's scarf as a souvenir.

LOFOTEN RAID

(*Below*) Fire raging at Stamsund, as British troops leave.

resistance in Norway by terrorism. This fact was also borne out by the German documents which were discovered at the military harbour control post at Svolvær, which proved 'how the Norwegian people have refused to collaborate in the organization of tyranny and how Germany, despite her installation of a rule of Gestapo terrorism, still fears the resentment of a subject people'. These documents revealed the devilish mentality of the Nazis, their calculated, callous methods of operation, but from the darkness a ray of hope emerges: the Germans, in these documents, admit that the Norwegians have opposed them very actively, and are still doing so in increasing intensity. On the 13th December, 1940,[1] the German Commander-in-Chief, Von Falkenhorst, wrote the following: 'Appearances would indicate that the temper and attitude of the Norwegian population have recently stiffened against our endeavours. For this reason it has become necessary, and it is more than ever urged, that restraint and caution be exercised.' This recognition of the failure of his mission is very significant, since these words were written in the darkest months of the year. Since then the resistance has daily increased, even though the oppression has become more rigorous than ever.

The soul of the Norwegian people is becoming steeled against the onslaught of the powers of darkness. Even life, man's most treasured possession, they are now ready to sacrifice willingly in the cause of freedom, and to win back a civilized form of life.

If the Germans had really been a Nordic people, as they falsely pretend to be, they would have understood that the secret clue to the soul of these people is their burning love of liberty and their respect for human and moral values.

[1] See Appendix 6, p. 151.

CONCLUSION

The Spirit of the Sea

I HAVE had many disappointments since the 9th April. Some people, in whom I firmly believed, have proved not so strong as I expected them to be, but most people have, on the other hand, proved to be stronger, more courageous, and faithful than I could have believed possible. To quote a Norwegian who has just arrived in Canada from Norway, having travelled round the world to get there: 'Now it is the most intense conviction of everyone that no sacrifice is too great for freedom. In former days when speeches were made on 17th May, Norway's Independence Day, many people thought that "liberty" was only a catchword, but now everyone is convinced that liberty is a condition of life. Ask the overwhelming majority of the youth of to-day about liberty, and witness how, not with words alone but by their actions, carried even to the extent of sacrificing their lives, they will acclaim it.

'In the beginning when this calamity suddenly overwhelmed us, we had a very deep respect for values: the mere threat that whole towns would be wiped out was enough to effect the surrender of any town, since the inhabitants believed that only in this way could they save and preserve the others. Now, however, we think quite differently: why try to save anything material—towns, houses, and so on—since the Germans will take them in any case, and by surrendering we lose all—including freedom of speech and liberty itself. We had had our liberty for so long that we had forgotten to appreciate its value. There is no people for whom liberty is such an essential condition of life.'

I believe even more to-day in my own people than ever before in my life. I will never forget that wonderful time during the summer and autumn of 1940, when our people found its soul and began the strong resistance. This resistance is now so great that King Haakon in a broadcast from London felt compelled to give a solemn warning against rash and premature actions, for fear that the movement might flare up into an open revolt which would give the Germans the opportunity to take brutal reprisals on a large scale.

I am afraid the Norwegian people will suffer both spiritually and materially even more in 1941 than they did last year. They will experience want and privation, distress and hunger and yet they will not yield. They will be pressed on all sides by the enemy, but they will stand up to it valiantly. They have preserved their sense of dignity and honour, and they can still laugh, and in this way weaken the German morale, which is suffering greatly in occupied Norway. The Norwegians are sound, and the present ordeal will strengthen them; they will never give up the fight because they realize at last what they have to fight against—Nazidom—and Norwegians will never become Nazi slaves.

Even after all the defeats and reversals of last year, and this year, they have an unyielding faith and absolute confidence in victory. They are optimistic because they firmly believe in their ideals and are convinced that the British Empire, backed by the vast material resources and steadily increasing moral support of the United States, will finally crush and defeat the devilish work of Adolf Hitler. They fully understand what Winston Churchill told his people and his allies when he said that they had to conquer or die. They also believe in a 'New Order' built upon democracy and justice, and the ideals of Fridtjof Nansen, the great scholar, explorer and humanitarian, whose titanic work in helping suffering people everywhere, without regard to nationality, creed, or race, can truly be looked on as the finest chapter in world history of the period following the first World War.

The British and the Norwegians are seafaring peoples. Their lives express the spirit of the sea. They are the true children of liberty, therefore they will fight for liberty to the bitter end, and they will sacrifice everything in order that the dark shadows of Nazidom shall be banished for ever.

The Original Letter of the Presidential Board to the King.
22nd June, 1940

After Oslo and the surrounding districts were occupied by the German troops on 9th April and the following days, and Mr. Vidkun Quisling in the absence of the Government had felt himself justified in forming a government, Norwegians of all classes and occupations in the occupied area considered it necessary to establish some arrangement during the occupation which would safeguard the population against unnecessary suffering and at the same time retain the King and his Council as the sole government of the country. Therefore, with the approval of the German authorities, the Administrative Council was appointed on 15th April to conduct the civil administration in the occupied areas. Attempts were made beforehand to get in touch with Your Majesty in order to get this arrangement endorsed. When this proved impossible, the Supreme Court considered that it should appoint the Council.

This step created orderly conditions and has given the population such security as is possible in the prevailing circumstances.

Since the whole country is occupied by German troops and the King and Government have left the country, the question has arisen of changing this arrangement.

On the 13th June the Administrative Council was advised of the New Order which was being considered by the Germans. Their proposal was that the Storting should be summoned immediately and should pass a resolution in accordance with an agenda in which point 1 referred to the dismissal of the Nygaardsvold Government; point 2, the deposition of the Royal House (reasons were to be drafted in greater detail); point 3, a declaration that the mandates of all members of parliament who are abroad are invalid; point 4, a decision regarding the confiscation of the property of those who make valid rights which are in opposition to points 1, 2, and 3; point 5, the choice of a new constitutional government; point 6, decisions regarding the postponement of new elections to the Storting—although not for longer than three months after the conclusion of peace; point 7, full powers for the government, including full powers to appoint new parliamentary representatives to the vacant seats. After these decisions had been taken the German Reichskommissar was to make known decisions of the Fuehrer to the effect that the Reichskommissar for the Occupied Area was to be recalled, and that there was to be appointed a special plenipotentiary (*Sendemann*) to look after German interests in the state known as 'The Kingdom of Norway'.

The German representative mentioned that points 1 and 2 in the agenda were final, although it would be possible to negotiate regarding the form of them. It was demanded that a decision should be taken by 8 p.m. on 17th June.

The members of the Presidential Board of the Storting who were able to be present have therefore, since 14th June, been assembled in Oslo together with representatives from the four main political parties and the trade union, and have had consultations partly together with the Administrative Council and representatives of industry. The Lord Chief Justice of the Supreme Court and the Bishop of Oslo have also been present at a number of the meetings.

On Saturday, 15th June, it was unanimously agreed to appoint Lord Chief Justice Berg, Bishop Berggrav, and District Magistrate Harbek to conduct negotiations on the basis of an arrangement which would not be in conflict with our constitution. On Saturday evening they advanced a proposal for an arrangement according to which the Supreme Court would appoint a State Council which would take over the functions of the government as far as internal administration was concerned. The Storting would then be summoned to approve the appointment of the State Council and to grant the latter the necessary full powers.

In conformity with their negotiating mandate, they rejected the demands that the Storting should depose the Royal House and the Government.

The Norwegian proposal was not accepted by the Germans, and it was clear that further negotiations on the basis of the negotiator's mandate could not lead to any result. The rest of the negotiations were then taken over by the members of the Presidential Board of the Storting who were present, strengthened by representatives of the Right and the Agrarian Parties. After further discussion a new proposal was submitted on Sunday evening, 16th June, according to which the Storting was to appoint a State Council which would temporarily take over those functions which the Constitution have imposed on the Monarchy. The question of the final settlement of the country's administration was to stand over until the conclusion of peace.

This proposal was also declared unacceptable by the Germans. On the 17th June, a German plan was produced which contained the same decision regarding the establishment of a State Council as in the Norwegian proposal. In addition it was demanded that the Storting should pass a declaration to the effect that the Nygaardsvold Government no longer enjoyed the confidence of the Storting and could therefore no longer be accepted as a government, and finally it was demanded that the Storting should approve a request to the King to the effect that he should relinquish his constitutional functions on behalf of himself and his House. Should an answer to this request not be received within two weeks, the State Council would take over the functions of the Monarchy.

When the report of France's capitulation was received, a solution was suggested from the Norwegian side, according to which peace negotiations would be begun between Norway and Germany, and the position of the Monarchy would be decided after the conclusion of peace. But this too did not lead to anything.

After further deliberations during the evening of Monday, 17th June, and into the night, followed by further discussions on the next day, the Presidential Board of the Storting (Magnus Nilssen, Moseid, Neri Valen, and Thorvik), supplemented by Lykke as a representative of the Right, came to the conclusion that they would have to agree to the presentation of a request to the King that he should relinquish his Constitutional functions on behalf of himself and his House.

The agreement, which was reached in the manner described, reads as follows :—

1. The full powers which were given to the Nygaardsvold Government at the meeting of 9th April are inoperative.

2. The Nygaardsvold Government can no longer be recognized as a government.

3. As the King is outside the country's borders, he is unable to exercise his constitutional functions.

4. The State Council takes over until further notice the government's activities and the King's constitutional functions.

New elections to the Storting are postponed until after the conclusion of peace and the State Council is charged with arranging new elections as soon as conditions permit, but at the latest three months after the conclusion of peace.

5. Those members of the Storting who are at present abroad will not be summoned during the remainder of the Storting's period of office, and will not be given an opportunity to take part in the meetings.

6. Until the new elections the State Council will have full powers in accordance with point 4 to take all steps which are necessary for the country's welfare.

7. Norway's constitutional form of government as a Kingdom shall be retained in the future.

As will be appreciated, it is unfortunately the Germans unalterable condition for this agreement that the King shall accede to the request that he should relinquish his constitutional functions on behalf of himself and his House.

Throughout the negotiations we have done everything possible to retain our popularly elected Royal House. All those who have participated in our deliberations, including all the representatives of the four main parties, have unanimously kept to this point of view, both because we were full of gratitude to the King and his House, and because we considered that this course would best safeguard our Constitution and the country's future. If, having failed to get this demand accepted, we have after all found it necessary to agree to the arrangement referred to above, it is because we saw in it the only way of avoiding unimaginable consequences of a kind to which we considered it would be inexcusable to expose the country and the people, and which would be decisive for the country's future.

We know with certainty what feelings this communication

of ours will arouse in the Norwegian spirit. But having regard to the people's welfare and the country's future, we have had to bow down before the inescapable consequences of the events that have taken place.

Trusting that Your Majesty will understand our motives, we beg to be informed of Your Majesty's decision by ...... July.[1]

---

[1] The date was not yet decided.

2

*Letter from the Presidential Board of the Storting to the King,
Oslo, 27th June, 1940*

After Oslo and the surrounding districts were occupied by German troops on the 9th April and the following days, and Mr. Vidkun Quisling, in the absence of the Government had felt himself justified in forming a government, Norwegians of all classes and occupations in the occupied area considered it necessary to establish some arrangement during the occupation which would safeguard the population against unnecessary suffering. Therefore, with the approval of the German occupation authorities, the Administrative Council was appointed on 15th April to conduct the civil administration in the occupied areas. Attempts were made beforehand to get in touch with Your Majesty in order to get this arrangment endorsed. When this proved impossible, the Supreme Court considered that it should appoint the Council.

This step helped to create orderly conditions and has given the population such security as is possible in the prevailing circumstances.

After the whole country was occupied by German troops, and the King and Government had left the country, the question arose of changing this arrangement. Those members of the Presidential Board of the Storting who were able to be present have therefore been assembled in Oslo since the 14th June, together with representatives of the four main political parties and the trade union confederation, and have had consultations, partly in conjunction with the Administrative Council.

On the basis of these discussions between the above-mentioned representatives, the following arrangement has been made with the German authorities :

'As the King and his government are outside Norway and are therefore prevented from carrying out those functions imposed on them by the Constitution, the Presidential Board of the Storting considers it to be its duty to the country and people to appoint a State Council.

'Parliament is therefore summoned to give its assent to this step and to pass detailed resolutions regarding the State Council's powers in matters regarding the country's administration.

The Presidential Board of the Storting will submit to the Storting a proposal to pass the following resolutions :—

1. The full powers which were given to the Nygaardsvold Government at the meeting of 9th April are inoperative.

2. The Nygaardsvold Government can no longer be recognized as a government.

3. As the King is outside the country's borders he is unable to exercise his constitutional functions.

Note.—On this point the Presidential Board reports that (in view of the situation) it has represented to the King that he should relinquish his constitutional functions on behalf of himself and his House.

4. The State Council takes over until further notice the government's activities and the King's constitutional functions. New elections to the Storting are postponed until after the conclusion of peace and the State Council is charged with arranging new elections as soon as conditions permit, but at the latest three months after the conclusion of peace.

5. Those members of the Storting who at present are abroad will not be summoned during the remainder of the Storting's period of office and will not be given an opportunity to take part in the meetings.

6. Until the new elections, the State Council will have full powers in accordance with point 4 to take all steps which are necessary for the country's welfare.

7. Norway's constitutional form of government as a Kingdom shall also be retained in the future.'

As will be appreciated, it is a condition of this arrangement that the King relinquishes his constitutional functions on behalf of himself and his House.

Having in mind the people's welfare and the country's future, we are forced, however painful it may be to us as Norwegian patriots, to direct an earnest prayer to your Majesty to respond to our appeal in this matter.

Trusting that Your Majesty will understand our motives,

we beg to be informed of Your Majesty's decision at the latest by 12th July.

With deep respect,

MAGNUS NILSSEN,
GABRIEL MOSEID,
P. THORVIK,
NERI VALEN, and
IVAR LYKKE *(appointed to the Presidential Board by the Right group)*.

3

The King's Answer to the Presidential Board of the Storting, 8th July, 1940

I have received the address of 27th June, 1940, from the Presidential Board of the Storting and have in complete comprehension of my personal responsibility and of the seriousness of the situation, conscientiously considered the decision so fateful to our country, which is dealt with in the letter of the Presidential Board.

I came to Norway in 1905, at the call of the Norwegian people, and I have during the years that have passed since then, to the best of my ability, tried to fulfil the duties that were thereby laid upon me.

My new country became infinitely dear to me, and I became devotedly attached to the Norwegian people. As always in the past, my motto 'Everything for Norway', is determining my actions, and could I be convinced that I in this moment could serve my people best by resigning my royal office, or could I feel sure that the Presidential Board of the Storting in this case were supported by a majority of the Norwegian people, I would—however deeply it would grieve me to separate from Norway—follow the appeal addressed to me by the Presidential Board.

I understand from the letter of the Presidential Board that the motion that the Presidential Board intend to present to the Storting has been prepared according to an agreement with the German authorities of occupation in Norway. The motion, therefore, is no expression of a free Norwegian resolution, but the result of constraint exercised by foreign military occupation forces.

I further understand from the letter that the members of the Storting, who have avoided the occupation forces by establishing their residence outside Norway, are not to be allowed to take part in the meetings, where the decision shall be taken with regard to the motion in question.

The Storting of 1814 acted upon an entirely opposite

principle, as it refused to approve the mandates of members who met from districts occupied by foreign military forces. This decision was based on the logical view that such an occupation would prevent the members from voting freely. In the *present* situation the representatives, including even the President of the Storting, who can still vote freely, are to be excluded from the Storting, while members who live under the pressure of foreign forces, shall all alone decide upon the destiny of the country.

I would betray my constitutional duties by sanctioning a resolution which may be passed by a Storting summoned under such circumstances.

The motion of the Presidential Board states in article 3 : 'As the King is outside Norway, he is unable to exercise his constitutional functions.'

Article 11 of Norway's Constitution expressly states that the King may stay up to six months outside Norway without the consent of the Storting and *with* such consent even longer. If the King is abroad *in the field*, the provision of article 41 of the Constitution seems to indicate that such consent could be dispensed with.

At the meeting of the Storting at Elverum on 9th April, 1940, the President stated, with the unanimous concord of the Storting, that the King and the Government could reside outside Norway if they found it necessary in order to exercise their powers freely and independently, and no limit of time was then intimated. There is consequently no constitutional foundation for the assertion that I cannot exercise the functions laid upon me by our Constitution.

The present Norwegian Government, under the leadership of Prime Minister Nygaardsvold, was appointed on 19th March, 1935; the composition of this Government has since then been somewhat changed, and recently so by the appointment of ministers belonging to other political parties than the one from which the Government originally came. A national Government has thereby been created, enjoying the unanimous confidence of the Storting, expressly signified by its resolution of 9th April, 1940.

According to Norwegian constitutional practice the Storting has full right to withdraw a vote of confidence already given; but this must in that case be done by a Storting acting in complete constitutional liberty and which has not arbitrarily been deprived of a number of its members. None of these conditions can be fulfilled by the assembly that is now to be summoned by the Presidential Board.

In the agreement between the Presidential Board and the German occupation authorities it is stated also that the Norwegian Government can no more exercise their constitutional powers, because they are residing outside Norway. I and the Government have no higher desire but to exercise our functions in Norway; it is only the presence of a foreign power that has compelled the Government, together with me, to leave the country temporarily. We have taken this step in conformity with the resolution of the Storting in order to maintain, so far as possible, a free and independent Norwegian management of public affairs.

If such conditions could be created in Norway that would permit me and the Government to return to the country in order to continue there our work in complete liberty, we would immediately do so. The obvious condition for such a step would be that all foreign military forces should leave the country. The arrangement with the German occupation forces that the Presidential Board has made implies, however, that the German occupation is still to be maintained, and in these circumstances I see no possibility of the existence of a free Norwegian Government within the limits of Norway.

In the motion of the Presidential Board it is stated that new elections for the Storting can only take place 'after the conclusion of peace', and this statement implies that Norway cannot get peace until the war between the Great Powers has been brought to an end. With regard to this supposition the Presidential Board is no doubt right, but then it is also evident that the proposed arrangement will not help the people of Norway to get the peace it is so strongly looking for.

Neither will the agreement with the German occupation forces help to promote the many economic interests that are so essential for the welfare of the people. I want you to bear in mind what the German demands to the Norwegian Government during the attack on the country on the night of 9th April, 1940, aimed at, i.e. the complete economic isolation of Norway, so far as her relations with all Western countries in and outside Europe were concerned. Important economic interests would, under a new Government, as planned by the appointment of a 'Riksraad' (State Council), suffer even more than now, as it would not be able to administer the vital interests of Norway abroad, which are now attended to by the present Government.

I will further point to an aspect of the matter under consideration, which throws a sharp light on the arrangement in question, and which is not mentioned in the letter of the Presidential Board. I refer to the extent of the authority invested in the planned 'State Council'. I will not go further into the fact, which is obvious to everybody, that the State Council in its management of public affairs will have to follow German direction so long as the occupation of Norway is upheld; but I will emphasize what is evident by the decision, which has recently been published by the German Government in Berlin, that no foreign States may maintain diplomatic representation in Oslo, and that Norway's foreign policy will be directed from the Ministry for Foreign Affairs in Berlin.

It is thereby clearly said that the new 'State Council' in Oslo does not represent an independent country, but only a German dependency. Consequently, an abdication on my part would not even formally be advantageous to an independent administration of public affairs in Norway; the 'State Council' would not be empowered with all the constitutional functions vested in the King.

I cannot see that the Presidential Board has any constitutional authority for redrafting legal resolutions voted so far by the Storting. On the contrary, it is quite evident that the whole arrangement proposed is unconstitutional.

I fail to see how I would act in the interests of our country by consenting to the request presented to me by the Presidential Board, whereby I would accept an arrangement, which is at variance with Norway's Constitution and which the foreign power in occupation forcibly tries to impose upon the Norwegian people.

I would thereby depart from the principle which, during my whole reign, has governed my actions, namely, a strict adherence to the Constitution.

The freedom and independence of the Norwegian people

is to me the first commandment of our Constitution, and I feel that I follow this commandment and best serve the interests of the Norwegian people in holding fast by the position and the task a free people gave me in 1905.

HAAKON.

4

The New Order in Norway

Reichskommissar Terboven's Speech, 25th September, 1940

We are living in the midst of an era in which decisions of inconceivable magnitude will be taken. They will give to Europe a completely new face and they will direct the development of society into entirely new channels which will be decisive for centuries to come.

There is no doubt that it is only a minority in each nation which fully understands how wide-embracing and how far-reaching are the events of to-day.

This applies particularly to those nations that were brought up to a wholly Western European, so-called democratic, mode of thought, under the influence of a government which was chained to the plutocratic forces, and a press which was in league with international capitalism. The great majority of these people were no longer aware how closely they had become bound to the spirit and attitude of mind of the plutocratic system, which was tending to become—and to a certain extent had already become—their second nature, in spite of the fact that this was in every way in conflict with their true interests.

Thus the more they became a part of this system, the cooler they became towards the German people. Those who benefited by this, easily transformed this coolness into a spirit of hostility. Thus each attempt to understand the German people, the great people in the middle of Europe, was deliberately hindered.

The greater part of these people knew, therefore, little or nothing about the German people, their thoughts, capabilities and interests, their will to live and powerful vitality, and when the German people supported National-Socialism, they accepted without criticism the usual expression 'Nazi Germany' as the name of an unnatural and worthless system, and adopted this judgment as their own opinion without having tested it.

There is therefore nothing curious in the fact that the majority of these nations stand perplexed in the face of present events. They appear dazed and allow the tremendous happenings to roll by in the vague hope—which again only proves their complete lack of understanding—that nevertheless some kind of miracle will one day occur, and all will return to the old rhythm which they liked so much because it was so comfortable.

There is nothing remarkable in that, because the previous rulers, who have nearly all fled, have seen to it that the people know nothing of such developments. These rulers now sit in London around a princely table, which England finances with the gold she has stolen from their people.

What do the majority of the people of Norway know for example about the German people and the path they have followed, let us say only in the last thirty years. At best a quantity of facts—the outbreak of war, the Armistice of 1918, the Versailles Treaty, the occupation of the Ruhr, the National-Socialist revolution and suchlike.

The Norwegian people have not, and cannot have, the slightest idea of all that the German people have gone through and suffered, of which these facts are just an outward sign. I have just explained the reasons for this.

Under such conditions the Norwegian leaders could easily conduct a policy of entire dependence on England—one that automatically placed Norway in the situation in which she found herself on the 9th April of this year.

The history of the world gives us many examples showing that a people which is in this manner surprised by fate can be washed away in a flood of events and buried for ever, unless men arise with better political sense than the masses have and can have, and who are courageous enough to step out along new paths even though to begin with those paths are strange and full of obstacles.

To-day a definite chapter in Norwegian political development is coming to its close. That is why I must now introduce a number of important and decisive measures.

This is the first time I have spoken publicly since 1st June of this year, and I do so in order to emphasize as strongly as possible how important are the regulations which have been made and will be made. I also do so for another reason, which I consider to be even more important.

I feel it is my duty and I consider it particularly urgent now to give the Norwegian people a clear and sober picture of the political situation at this moment, and of the causes and circumstances which have led to this situation and the regulations which I consider to be necessary.

It was on the 9th June of this year that the Englishmen hurriedly departed from the last piece of Norwegian soil, and the remainder of the Norwegian forces, which had been betrayed in every possible way, were forced to capitulate. Thus Norwegian unity was re-established and the whole country was protected by German arms.

At the same time, the King and the Nygaardsvold Government fled from the country together with the Englishmen and went to London, which at that time still appeared to be a safe place. This created a completely new political situation for the Norwegian people.

It was then that people from the Administrative Council and the political parties approached me and asked me to agree to the planning and negotiation of a New Political Order in Norway. It was to be built on political realities which were now clear and unambiguous.

Had I, at that moment, seen the matter only from the point of view of what was—morally and politically—correct and not reckoned with the fact that for years the greater part of the people had been led astray, that they had been deliberately misinformed, so that they were not able without further ado to tear themselves away from an attitude caused by old habits—then it would have been simple enough to answer, without fear of rebuttal:

Gentlemen: The Norwegian people whom you have governed have had to learn the hard and bitter language of experience. You now realize that a New Political Order must appear in Norway, which is built on the given political realities, or in other words: You will take it upon yourselves to bring about a complete revolution in the fundamental principles of Norwegian policy, which has been based on the desire to be entirely subservient to the Englishmen, and transform it in such a way that it will be possible to initiate honourable and lasting co-operation with the Great German Reich. In the name of all that is reasonable you cannot deny that, in the truest sense of the phrase, this would be to 'set the cat to watch the cream'.

It was you and your parties that, in the years that have passed, led the Norwegian people into an incomparable political, economic, and spiritual dependence on the English plutocracy.

It was you and your parties that, like other lackies, stood ready at the slightest hint from England, to misuse your own people for all kinds of mercenary work, to make difficulties for the authoritarian states, either through the League of Nations or by other means.

It was you and your parties that actively supported the criminal policy conducted by the emigrant Nygaardsvold Government, or positively tolerated it, thus preparing the way for that policy which the Norwegian people must now answer for with all the bitterness which follows a lost war and perhaps with even worse. You cannot escape the fact that you must be responsible for this policy and its consequences, because as recently as 9th April you all supported the unanimous resolution of the Storting which gave the Nygaardsvold Government extraordinary full powers to conduct war against Germany.

On the other side, we have a national, political organization, the National Union (*Nasjonal Samling*). Since it began its political activities, it has untiringly, openly and honestly followed two basic political principles:

1. Norway must expand its military strength, so that it can successfully defend its neutrality if necessary. It is treachery that the Nygaardsvold Government deliberately undermines this military strength. 2. Norwegian policy must tear itself away from dependence on England. Norway's position and the great future which lies before the Great German Reich definitely demands that Norway shall seek co-operation with the Great German brother people.

Had you politicians of the old parties accorded proper recognition to these two principles, then Norway to-day would have been a free land, a land at peace! Documents which are well known to all give undeniable proof of this.

But now that you and your parties are prepared to recognize

'National Union', and the political principles of the 'National Union', what is more natural than to let the 'National Union' take over the political leadership in this country? 'National Union' has certainly a moral and political right to it, and all the more so since you have 'seen the matter in a new light'—even though very late.

As I remarked before, that would have been the simplest answer to give and at the same time an answer which would have been politically and morally incontrovertible.

But I did not take that course. On the contrary, I gave my assent to a request that I should draw up proposals based on the declaration made in my speech of 1st June of this year, a declaration by which I still stand, as far as it concerns the Norwegian people.

I said on that occasion:

'There is nothing in the past which can give grounds for creating insurmountable barriers between the Norwegian and the German peoples.

'The German people hold out their hands to the Norwegian people, honourably, straightforwardly, and without reservations; they are willing to co-operate as comrades on a basis of mutual respect.

'May those men who feel their responsibility as leaders of the Norwegian people, understand the signs of the times!'

In addition, I gave my assent for the following reasons:

1. In the past the political and economic leaders in Norway had directed the attention of the people entirely towards England, whereas with regard to Germany, especially National Socialist Germany, they had knowingly and purposely given incorrect information, lied and instilled into the people an attitude of mind which made it very difficult for them to achieve in one jump the fundamental re-orientation which was necessary.

The German people was never unfavourably disposed towards the Norwegian people, and is not so disposed to-day. As a matter of fact it feels tied to Norway as part of the great Nordic family, and emphasizes the need to work with it in friendship and with reciprocal respect. But this declaration of friendship is only of value when it is not one-sided.

Therefore I have taken the responsibility solely for the sake of the Norwegian people, of seeing that no road should be closed in advance which might enable the passage to the necessary new orientation to take on such a form as would make it easier for the Norwegian people to embark on the new road.

2. Secondly, I considered it absolutely essential for the future political development and in order to clarify the real political situation, that the New Order should be introduced by a 'mea culpa' declaration by the old political parties.

3. Finally, I was quite certain that these negotiations, whether they ended positively or negatively, would give the Norwegian people an excellent object lesson about the political morals of the leading forces in the old parties, and show them to what an extent they were prepared to betray their own political past and all that they had always presented to the people as holy and unshakable.

In this connection it is my duty to make the following unambiguous declaration:

Despite the fact that 'National Union' had without doubt both the political and the moral right to take over the reins of government, the movement did not make that demand, and on the contrary acted with remarkable discipline and self-control, for the reason which I mentioned above.

National Union was the last group to oppose anything which could make it easier for the great masses of the people to understand the inevitable new orientation and which could prevent the creation, through ignorance and misinformation, of new political antagonisms which would in any case be overcome in the near future, but which would, for the time being, cause the people deep wounds, whereas the way ought to be clear and clean.

At the same time, Quisling and his men were not for one moment in doubt about the position of the old political parties, what they thought and how they behaved. Nobody can confirm this better than I can. It was in these circumstances that the negotiations took place and continued with short breaks up to these last few days.

Last Tuesday I broke them off completely. Perhaps many honest Norwegians will now breathe freely and say: Then our old political leaders have been so full of character that they have defended the things which they represented to the people as almost holy and never to be touched—the King and his House and the Constitution—things which they had on their lips almost daily. This was all the easier for them because there was no one who forced them to negotiate, but they did it of their own free will.

Unfortunately I must destroy this dream with facts and documents as fundamental, as comprehensive and as clear as it is possible to get them.

The Presidential Board of the Storting, together with the leaders of the four old parties—Left, Right, Agrarian and Labour—has voluntarily declared itself willing to carry through, and has pledged itself in writing, to the following New Political Order:

1. The King and his House are deposed and deprived of all Constitutional functions.

2. The full powers which the Storting gave to the Nygaardsvold Government on 9th April of this year, are declared to be invalid.

3. The Nygaardsvold Government is deposed.

4. A State Council is to be formed, composed of fifteen members.

5. This State Council receives full powers to take all measures which the well-being of the country demands and shall, therefore, have transferred to it the King's, the Government's, and the Storting's Constitutional functions. But it is not only the Presidential Board of the Storting and the old party leaders who have agreed to these points. Before they gave me their pledge, which they signed, they had ascertained by means of preliminary votes in all party groups that there were assured and qualified majorities for the measures named—even though from the Storting's point of view the measures were taken in accordance with the constitutional emergency powers and therefore would not have required a two-thirds majority. They have also given me written reports regarding these preliminary divisions.

It is true that I was asked to give my pledge on the following point:

I should declare myself agreeable that the Storting should place one point on the Agenda in the form of a motion.

This point read:

'The Mandates of Members of Parliament are valid until a new General Election has taken place.'

I agreed to this point being included in the motion in spite of the fact that the four parliamentary parties considered that the Storting's legislative period expired at the latest by December of this year:

1. Because it had no political significance, as the Storting at the same time unconditionally transferred their Constitutional functions to the State Council.

2. Because in this manner Parliament itself gave the people a really wonderful object lesson in the value of parliamentarianism as a principle and in its practical workings. For in this way the people got to know, or they know now, how a parliament is prepared—if necessary—to throw everything overboard—the monarchy, the government, the constitution, yes, even its own political existence—not because they have suddenly begun to understand the New Order—that would indeed be unlikely, though all honour to them if they did—but obviously in order to save from the onward sweeping political storm the thing which was certainly the most important for them, namely their own material existence.

One can only describe it as a political association which is politically corrupt through and through, individually and as a whole.

This measure was, as I have stated earlier, already accepted by parliament de facto, morally and politically, with at least a two-thirds majority. The reason why these theatricals were not displayed on the parliamentary stage is wholly because I on my side broke off the negotiations.

During the negotiations and the formulation of the parliamentary motion, it had been a guiding principle that the State Council should operate on its own responsibility. In opposition to this, attempts were now made with the help of legal subterfuges to bring the decisive influence in the State Council into the hands of the old parties. A final warning about this from my side was apparently not heeded. It was then that I broke off the negotiations.

This leads me to the consequences which flow from this situation and to the measures which have become necessary.

1. The Royal House has no longer any political importance and will not return to Norway—even more so as the Storting has deposed it by a two-thirds majority.

2. The same applies to the Nygaardsvold Government which has also fled.

3. It naturally follows that all activity in accord with or in favour of the Royal House or the emigré government is forbidden.

4. The activity of the Administrative Council is at an end.

5. Under the power granted me by the Fuehrer's decree of 24th April of this year, I have appointed the following [1] constituted State Councillors, who from to-day have taken over the leadership of the Government's activities:

(1) Trade, industry, crafts and fisheries: Sigurd Halvorsen Johannessen, Trade Adviser.

(2) Shipping : Captain Kjeld Irgens.

(3) Church and Education: Ragnar Skancke, Professor.

(4) Home Office: Wiljelm Hagelin, Director.

(5) Department of Social Affairs: Professor Birger Meidell.

(6) Department of Supply: Öystein Ravner, Director.

(7) Department of Police: Jonas Lie, Police Chief.

(8) Department of Justice: Sverre Riisnæs, Public Prosecutor.

(9) Department of Agriculture: Thorstein Jon Onstad Fretheim, Veterinary Surgeon.

(10) Department of Finance: Erling Sandberg, Bank Chairman.

(11) Department of Public Enlightenment and Culture: Gulbrand Lunde, Director.

(12) Department of Sport: Axel Stang, Landowner.

(13) Department of Works: Tormod Hustad, Architect.

6. The old political parties have been dissolved to-day. Further details will be made known later.

7. New associations which have as their object the carrying on of any kind of political activity will not be tolerated.

It may seem to many at first glance that these steps are harsh. They have become necessary, and I have made quite clear their political and moral justification. I take it for granted that each worker, employee, and official in the public service will continue to do his duty to the best of his ability.

[1] In German, *Kommissarische Staträte* (Commissarial State Councillors), i.e. Councillors appointed by, and responsible only to, the German Reichs-kommissar Terboven.

K

On the other hand let no one doubt that I will punish any neglect of duty in the sternest manner—the interests of the whole people demand it.

Apart from that, these measures will only effect adversely those who show ill will.

Norwegian men and women!

The political development of recent years has shown quite clearly that the political principles of 'National Union' and its leader Vidkun Quisling have been correct. The Norwegian people would have been spared much suffering and distress if they had been favourably disposed towards this political doctrine and had not always been hindered from listening to it by the over-powerful old parties.

Nevertheless 'National Union' held its hand at a time when it had no other reason for doing so than this: that on no account must any road be blocked which might help the people to find their way to the New Political Order.

But it is important to state here that National Union would at no time have anything to do with the earlier negotiations. The responsibility for these negotiations rests entirely on the old parties.

The possibilities which I so obligingly allowed to be discussed are now dead, and I therefore declare firmly, seriously and emphatically: I am willing, now as before, to work together in a spirit of comradeship and with reciprocal appreciation with all those who on their side feel similarly towards the German people.

Now as before, I, and with me the German people, with the whole of their industrial resources, are willing to co-operate with all energy to rebuild the Norwegian economy, and I am certain that Norway has a great future before her within the framework of the New Order which is being formed in the European area (Raum).

But there is one thing about which the whole Norwegian people must now be absolutely clear: In order that the present political situation may be settled for the future in a Norwegian and a national way, so that the Norwegian people may regain their freedom and independence to the fullest extent, there is only one route and that leads through the N.S. (National Union).

It is now for the Norwegian people themselves to choose.

5

Norwegian Bishops' Letter of Protest, January, 1941

The very foundation of the Church of Norway rests on a definite constitutional relationship to the State, and on the assumption that the duty of the State and all departments of the government is to uphold righteousness and justice in accordance with the will of God. The Norwegian Constitution states: 'The Evangelical Lutheran religion shall be the official religion of Norway.' It therefore is imperative and essential that the Church should know clearly whether the State, which is also concerned with ecclesiastical matters, accepts and honours the legal and moral obligations contained in the Church's articles of faith and in the Bible. Such assurance is essential to the very being of the Church. It has thus been of the greatest importance, in view of what has happened since 9th April, that the overseers of the Church have been able to point out that justice has been maintained in accordance with the law of the land. This has been emphasized in several circulars issued by the Norwegian bishops. Thus the Bishop of Oslo, in an extensive pronouncement entitled 'The Temporal and the Eternal' (July, 1940), followed by each of the bishops in their writings of October and November, stated that our laws were being observed and that due respect should be given to all authorities.

Church authorities have hitherto been justified in taking this viewpoint when advising their ministers and congregations. For Hitler's proclamation of 24th April was in full accord with international law, while the Reichskommissar, in his talk of 1st June, declared acceptance of Article 46 of the Hague Convention which guarantees religious freedom, and later in his order of 28th September, asserted that the independence of the courts should not be touched.

The attitude of the Church, needless to say, is at all times governed by the basic principles outlined above: Norway's Constitution, the articles of faith and the Bible.

Recently, however, much serious doubt has arisen

concerning the validity of the statements made by the bishops to their church members. We are faced with the problem of whether the State and its departments will maintain order and justice as provided by our Church's articles of faith.

We point to three specific instances which, in substance, are interwoven and which bear out the contention that acts of violence, instead of being prevented, are actually condoned. That the fundamental principles of justice are being broken down is shown by the following concrete examples:—

1. The systematic rule of terror by the Nazi Storm Troopers.
2. The resignation of the Supreme Court of Norway.
3. Interference with the ministers' pledge of silence.

These accusations are supported by documentary evidence of which here are given brief resumes:—

1. The attack by Storm Troopers on the Oslo Business College, 30th November, during which teachers and the director were knocked down and severely assaulted, was in itself bad enough. But the seriousness of the event was increased by the slogan published that very morning by the official organ of the Nazi party: 'We shall strike again in such a way that they shall lose both sight and hearing. Storm troopers, close your ranks. He who hits us once shall be hit tenfold. This shall be our watchword.'

If a nation accepts such a watchword and refuses to uphold law and order, then it may truly be said that such a nation has abandoned the fundamental principles of law-abiding society. The problem takes on a much more serious aspect because we are here confronted with a series of entirely unprovoked incidents. We call attention to the brutal attack on the chairman of the Students Union at Trondheim on 29th November, and further, to the assault on an office-boy who was kidnapped in an automobile on the night of 11th December, stripped of his clothes and flogged by Storm Troopers. There have been similar incidents in Oslo and in other towns.

The gravity of this situation is increased by the fact that, so far, none of the culprits has been apprehended. On the contrary, the ranking official of 'law and order' issued a decree on 14th December instructing the police not only not to interfere in such incidents, but to give 'active support to the

Storm Troopers'. The revolting nature of these single acts of violence is such as to make them a problem which concerns the security of society as a whole.

In addition, there is the circular sent out by the Department of the Interior on 16th December, in which all state and municipal employees are ordered actively to support the Storm Troopers. Any refusal will be looked upon as an 'action inimical to the state' and will give rise to 'drastic punishment'.

If such things should continue systematically, the Church's servants will feel the lack of any basis for guiding the conscience of the people in so far as respect and confidence in the law of the land are concerned. Therefore we beg to lay the foregoing documented facts before the head of our Church Department.

2. The second set of facts, which must reluctantly be linked with the above, relates to the insecurity which church members feel since the Supreme Court of Norway has abandoned its duties.

The Supreme Court has asserted that the Justice Department's decree of 14th November, whereby the departmental chief is given authority to discharge and appoint jurors, judges, and court clerks, constitutes an attack on law and order which is in open conflict with recognized principles of justice and which will lead to the most fateful consequences, since freedom of the courts—which is guaranteed by the Constitution—is of vital importance for security and justice. The very fact that all members of the highest court in the land have found it necessary to resign their duties is one that must needs create within the church a far-reaching feeling of insecurity with regard to the foundations of law and order in society.

Since, in the articles of faith, the Church upholds that which is legitimate in the State's actions, and since these articles call upon every Christian to be loyal to the State, the acting head of the Church and Education Department will certainly agree that it is the duty and the right of Church officials to speak up and request information on such serious matters as those just mentioned.

He will also understand that the seriousness of the situation will not diminish when we emphasize that violence breeds violence and that a spirit of hate is developing among the people. Not the least important is the way such things affect growing youth. The training of Christian character is by law assigned to church and school, and this constitutes one of the Church's main tasks. Therefore, when the Department of Church and Education, in a bulletin dated 12th November and addressed to all school officials, advises all responsible schoolmen to guarantee upon their honour that they will give positive and active support to every resolution and decree issued by the new authorities—then, we view the whole matter as approaching a conflict of conscience in the very essence of our profession.

3. Of the most vital concern to our calling is the newly-published order of the police department according to which the professional oath of silence of ministers can be abolished by the police. Our right to professional secrecy is not only guaranteed by law, but has always been a fundamental requirement in the Church calling when we minister to sorrow and receive confessions from people in trouble. It is of the utmost importance to the Church that people have full and unqualified confidence in the ministerial oath of silence, as it has been recognized both in Norwegian law and in the Church's decrees throughout all times and in all Christian lands.

To abolish this Magna Carta of the conscience is an attack upon the very heart of the Church. It is an attack which takes on an especially serious character by the fact that paragraph 5 empowers police to imprison an offending pastor and force him to talk without his having been taken before a court of law.

The above facts, together with other serious happenings which we do not touch upon here, have forced us to send this request for clarification to the Department of Church and Education, in the assurance that the difficulty of our situation will be met with understanding.

Signed by all Seven Norwegian Bishops.

(*Translation.*)
SECRET.

Harbour Control Post, Svolvaer

(Received 6th February, 1941)

OSLO, *December 13th*, 1940.

Field Post No. 07626.

From German Commander-in-Chief, Norway.

No. 2929/40 geh.

Appearances would indicate that the temper and attitude of the Norwegian population have recently stiffened against our endeavours. For this reason, it has become necessary, and it is more than ever urged, that restraint and caution be exercised.

I hereby renew my order that all members of the German Army (*Wehrmacht*) should abstain from all domestic Norwegian political controversy and not mix in discussions which are purely and solely the affair of the Norwegian population. Members of the *Wehrmacht* must not become involved in riots, assemblies, demonstrations, and brawls (literally " beatings up "), which have their origin in political causes. All members of the *Wehrmacht* must be firmly instructed on all such occasions to remove themselves at once from the scene of the incident, in order to avoid becoming involved as idle spectators in the discussion, and thereby placing themselves in an invidious position, vis-à-vis not only the Norwegians, but also the police units entrusted with the preservation of order.

Wherever Norwegian or German police units are within reach, it is their duty, and their duty alone, to take action according to special instructions issued to them.

In the event of no German or Norwegian police units being available, the Senior Army Officer should leave the political discussion to Norwegians. Action is to be taken by Units of the *Wehrmacht* only where the incident constitutes a threat to troops or Army property or constitutes a demonstration against the Occupying Power and the Fuehrer.

In such cases, however, *Military force should be brought into action in its full severity.* In this case it is absolutely necessary to avoid stringent action being compromised by individual members of the *Wehrmacht* becoming involved in the demonstrations, and thereby impeding the use of arms on the part of the troops.

Intervention by the German *Wehrmacht* must only occur in order to ensure *the security of the Occupying Force and its property, but where action is taken it must be ruthless and employ the severest measures.*

I once again urgently desire to impress upon all outposts and all local Senior officers the importance of proceeding as instructed above, and to send a detailed report of incidents such as those indicated above from their locality direct to the *Wehrmacht* Commander in Norway, Oslo, Division 1a, marked 'Special Incidents'.

(Signed) VON FALKENHORST,
Commander-in-Chief.

(From the Government White Paper: 'Secret German Documents seized during the Raid on the Lofoten Islands on 4th March, 1941.')